ROYAL NAVY
MOTOR GUN BOAT

1942–45 (British Power Boat Company)

First published in July 2020

A catalogue record for this book is available from the British Library.

ISBN 978 1 78521 142 3

Library of Congress control no. 2017949636

Published by Haynes Publishing,
Sparkford, Yeovil, Somerset BA22 7JJ, UK.
Tel: 01963 440635
Int. tel: +44 1963 440635
Website: www.haynes.com

Haynes North America Inc.,
859 Lawrence Drive, Newbury Park,
California 91320, USA.

Printed in China.

ROYAL NAVY MOTOR GUN BOAT

1942–45 (British Power Boat Company)

Owners' Workshop Manual

Insights into the design, construction, operation and restoration of MGB 81 – the 'Spitfire of the sea'

Stephen Fisher and Diggory Rose

The "Power" 71' 6" Motor Torpedo Boat joins the complement of the Royal Navy's warships.

The development and construction of the modern high speed motor boat into an efficient fighting vessel is one of the achievements of

THE BRITISH POWER BOAT COMPANY LTD.

Constructors of Scott-Paine designed Surface Craft

Contents

Introduction

When Britain declared war on Germany on 3 September 1939, it did not do so with the same range of 'little ships' of Coastal Forces that it would end the war with. Indeed, Coastal Forces didn't even exist as a separate division of the Royal Navy in 1939 and their handful of small boats were scattered around the globe. Twelve Motor Torpedo Boats (MTBs) made up the 1st Flotilla in Malta, while six more of the 2nd MTB Flotilla were in Hong Kong.

At home the situation was even worse and only a few experimental MTBs were in service at Portsmouth. The boat-building yards of Vosper in Portsmouth, Thornycroft at Hampton on Thames and the British Power Boat Company in Hythe, Hampshire, hurriedly completed the MTBs they were building for foreign navies that were quickly requisitioned by the Admiralty. The Malta flotilla was hastily recalled and, in January 1940, those that were still seaworthy were joined by three new boats of the 4th MTB Flotilla at Felixstowe. It was an inauspicious start to the war for the Royal Navy's Coastal Forces.

There were, however, a number of small

BELOW MGB 81 on trials after her 2018 refit. *(Portsmouth Naval Base Property Trust – PNBPT)*

boats of another type available at the outbreak of the war. At HMS *Osprey*, the Royal Navy's Anti-Submarine school at Portland, were six boats of the 1st Motor Anti-Submarine Boat (MA/SB) Flotilla. Although almost identical in appearance to MTBs, MA/SBs had been designed to intercept and engage enemy U-boats in Britain's coastal waters. In time they would evolve into something far more formidable, a boat that would truly turn the tide of the war waged in the North Sea and English Channel – the Motor Gun Boat (MGB).

The MGB is often eclipsed in history by the more famous MTB, and the more iconic image of Coastal Forces in the Second World War is of the renowned 70ft Vosper. MGBs are not as well known by comparison, although their contribution to the war was no less significant. Early MTBs were dedicated to torpedo attacks and only carried light gun armament, ostensibly for defence against aircraft. While powerful in the attack, especially against large merchant ships, MTBs were woefully inadequate to deal with craft of their own type. When German S-boats began to patrol Britain's home waters

and attack coastal convoys carrying vital war material around the country, the MTBs offered no defence. Their torpedoes were no use against small, nimble and shallow-draught boats, and their machine guns were insufficient to engage in surface actions with the more powerfully armed S-boats.

The MGB was the perfect vessel to fulfil this role instead. Originating from conversions of existing MA/SBs, in 1942 the first purpose-built gun boats, the 71ft 6in British Power Boat Mk V MGBs, came into service. With the high speeds of MTBs (approximately 40kts) the MGBs were fast enough to catch S-boats and, eschewing torpedoes for heavier gun armament, they could fight the German boats on their own terms. In fact, the Kriegsmarine was limited in the way it could respond to the gun boat. The S-boat's role was to attack merchant ships, much the same as the MTB – but they were too few in number to deploy in the same role that the MGB now fulfilled. While the Royal Navy had evolved to meet the needs of the warfare unfolding in the English Channel, the Kriegsmarine could not risk its fleet of torpedo boats in open surface combat to suppress the MGBs. By 1943, Coastal Forces had the upper hand in Britain's home waters.

The Mk V MGB had been designed at the British Power Boat Company by chief designer George Selman and, unlike any Coastal Forces boat before it, it provided a hull strong enough to survive the pounding waves of the English Channel and North Sea. Throughout

the 1940s not one of the 96 Mk V and Mk VI boats ever suffered any structural defects – they were near-perfect fast motorboats and could take the weight of heavy gun armament to boot. The MGB then evolved after experience in service showed that the hulls of the Mk V could also take the additional weight of two torpedo tubes. Essentially the MGBs could carry the weight of firepower of the MGB *and* the torpedo tubes of an MTB, hence the Mk V established the origins of the post-war multi-purpose Fast Patrol Boat.

It is ironic, then, that this marked the end of the MGB. In 1943 the Admiralty made the decision to reclassify all MGBs as MTBs (even those not equipped with torpedoes). All subsequent boats were completed as MTBs and the only MGBs that remained in service were some of the early MA/SB conversions and a handful of 'long' 115ft Fairmile Ds in the Mediterranean. It was not until after the war that all boats were reclassified as Fast Patrol Boats.

The MGB became remembered as a wartime expedient, overshadowed by the more famous MTB even though it was the former that had evolved to accommodate the offensive weapons of the torpedo boats. As the peacetime navy shrunk, the hundreds of Coastal Forces boats that had served in the war were sold off until none remained. Those that survived were converted to houseboats moored in estuaries and marinas around the UK.

It is very likely that, were it not for the determination of a few individuals, there would not be any capable of putting to sea today. Fortunately a handful have been saved, including one of the original purpose-built gun boats, MGB 81. Over the course of some 20 years this boat was returned to her original appearance after a post-war life as a pleasure craft and a houseboat. Now, preserved for the benefit of the nation, she is justifiably part of the country's National Historic Fleet.

BELOW A 1945 British Power Boat advertisement featuring the Mk VI Motor Torpedo Boat. *(Author's Collection)*

View point

Soon the appearance of British Power Boat M.T.B.'s, M.G.B.'s and Rescue Launches will be a less ubiquitous sight in western waters. But craft of new design will take their place . . .

the picket boats . . . seaplane tenders and custom launches of a world engaged in the vital tasks of re-establishing the threads of commerce throughout the seven seas.

THE BRITISH POWER BOAT COMPANY LTD.

CONSTRUCTORS OF SCOTT-PAINE SURFACE CRAFT

Acknowledgements

Writing a book about MGB 81 wouldn't have been possible without the support and assistance of a number of people involved with Coastal Forces and historic vessels. Although a lot of information about MGB 81's career has been gleaned from primary sources found in the National Archives and Naval Historical Branch, the work of past historians has been invaluable in piecing together her service history. In particular Geoffrey Hudson, historian for the Coastal Forces Heritage Trust, carried out detailed research in the 1990s that made the research for this book significantly easier.

Our grateful thanks go to all those who have kindly supplied expertise and images. These include Al Ross for permission to use drawings and photographs from his collection; Tim Deacon, David Fricker, Richard Hellyer, Richard de Kerbrech, Danny Lovell and Philip Simons for their photographs of historic boats taken over many years; Clive Kidd, Honorary Curator of the Collingwood Historic Collection (http://www.rnmuseumradarandcommunications2006.org.uk); Richard Basey of the MTB 102 Trust (www.mtb102.com); Jeremy and Jeffrey Ridgway, grandchildren of Hubert Scott-Paine; Peter Scott for the use of the photographs taken by his grandfather James William Yates who served on MGB 16; and Christopher Timms for permission to use the photographs of his father Roderick Timms who served in the 35th MTB Flotilla (www.rodericktimms.royalnavy.co.uk).

We are also grateful to those who have operated and serviced MGB 81 in recent years. These include: the staff and volunteers of Boathouse 4 who operate MGB 81, in particular Tiger Juden for his photographs, and the team at Berthon who serviced MGB 81 in 2017–18 and documented their work so thoroughly (more information on the refit can be found at www.berthon.co.uk/marine-services/casestudies/1942-mgb-81-gunboat).

Most importantly we thank the many veterans who have made their images available to the British Military Powerboat Trust and Portsmouth Naval Base Property Trust in the past, including John Lake and Robert Westwood; and all those involved in the British Military Powerboat Trust and Coastal Forces Heritage Trust, past and present, who kept the memory and spirit of these boats alive.

Every effort was made to contact those whose contributions are used in this book. We hope that the few we were not able to reach will see their inclusion as a tribute to the history of these small boats and their crews.

Chapter One

Origins of the MGB

The MGB was very much a wartime expedient, created in response to a German threat. But it evolved from a series of boats that had developed over the course of the previous 70 years, as new technologies and designs came together to create small vessels faster than anything on water before them.

OPPOSITE MTBs 100 and 102, two pre-war MTBs. *(Peter Scott)*

The birth of the Royal Navy's fast strike boats

The fast motorboat began life as a pleasure and sports boat in the tail end of the 19th century. For decades, engineers had realised that flat-bottomed (or 'hydroplane' hulls) would lift out of the water, reducing their resistance and increasing their speed. At the same time, this severely curtailed their stability and it wasn't until 1872 that the Reverend Charles Ramus of Sussex, experimenting with models, found that combining two planing hulls as wedges overcame the problem. Including steps on the underside of a flat-bottomed hull increased the points of contact with the water, maintaining the hull's lift and speed and simultaneously stabilising it.

Not long after this breakthrough, another technological development created sufficient power to exploit the hydroplane hull, when engineers like Gottlieb Daimler and Karl Benz perfected petrol-driven internal combustion engines. These engines were small, light and powerful, and when combined with a hydroplane hull, allowed small boats to travel across the water at greater speeds than had previously been possible. In 1902 the Motor

Yacht Club was founded and in 1903 a racing series, the British International Trophy, began. In 1908 the Olympics featured motorboat races – the one and only time in their history that powered boats have featured in the international competition. Three races were held on Southampton Water, two of which were won by *Gyrinus II*, a boat designed by Sir John Thornycroft.

Sport led the development of early fast boats but in the First World War, the concept of using such vessels as strike boats came to the fore. When three young officers considered possible ways to counter the raids made on the English coast by squadrons of the High Seas Fleet in the early years of the war, their thoughts turned to the racing boats they had seen in the early 1910s. In theory, their shallow draughts should allow them to skim over sandbars and minefields that had hitherto prevented conventional warships from easily approaching enemy bases.

The Admiralty were impressed with the idea and Thornycroft was employed to produce a suitable boat capable of carrying a single torpedo. Basing his design on his own racing boats, Thornycroft constructed a simple 40ft boat which, using a planing stepped hull and

BELOW *Miranda IV*, Thornycroft's pre-war racing boat that became the basis for the Coastal Motor Boat (CMB). *(Thornycroft, 1918)*

ABOVE **CMBs operating with the Grand Fleet during the First World War.** *(From a painting by W. Wyllie in* More Sea Fights of the Great War, *1919)*

a V8 or V12 engine, could achieve speeds of up to 35kts. To keep the boat light, somewhat unconventionally, the single torpedo was carried in a trough in the stern of the boat, but faced forwards. This way the whole boat could be aimed at the target and a simple ram system fired by a small explosive charge was used to push the 700kg weapon from the trough tail first. After it was launched the crew would need to turn aside quickly, lest the torpedo 'porpoised' as it picked up speed and ran into the back of them. The system sounded dramatic, but the boat would need to turn away from its target after attacking in any case, and in practice none was ever hit by its own torpedo in action.

By August 1916, 12 of the new boats, which were soon officially titled 'Coastal Motor Boats' (CMBs) were in service. They quickly proved themselves capable, sinking German destroyer *G88* in April 1917 and working effectively as minelayers close to the enemy coast. The following year CMBs played an important part in the Zeebrugge Raid, although their operations were not without loss. Several were sunk when raids on the Schillig Roads, on Germany's north coast, were carried out in 1918, and by the time of the Armistice in November 1918 nine CMBs had been lost to enemy action and four more to accidents.

Even after the fighting in western Europe ended in November 1918, CMBs continued to provide valuable service during the British intervention in the Russian Civil War. In June 1919, Lieutenant Augustus Agar used his CMB to torpedo and sink the Bolshevik cruiser *Oleg* and in August that year a flotilla of the boats raided the enemy harbour at Krondstadt near St Petersburg, largely incapacitating the Bolshevik Navy in the Baltic.

The success of the small CMBs in the latter years of the war and in Russia showed their promise. By no means, however, were the Royal Navy the only navy to demonstrate these vessels' potential – in June 1918 the Austro-Hungarian dreadnought battleship SMS *Szent István* was sunk by two torpedoes fired from the 52ft Italian torpedo boat MAS-15. Much like the invention of the torpedo itself in the 19th century, the CMB and its equivalents had shown that small and inexpensive fast boats could threaten traditional navies.

Unfortunately, the Admiralty did not see it that way. In the post-war period, the Royal Navy shrank to a peacetime force and the CMBs were seen as an unnecessary extravagance with limited potential. In 1920 the Admiralty cancelled any outstanding orders for CMBs and the following year their purpose-built base at Osea Island, Essex, was closed. Of

the 116 CMBs that had been built, only a few were retained for trials and torpedo testing. It might nearly have been the end of the small strike boat in the Royal Navy, were it not for the forward-thinking attitude of some of the country's private boatbuilders.

The British Power Boat Company

Hubert Scott-Paine was a great entrepreneur of the early 20th century. One of the original founders of the Supermarine aviation company, he had taken overall ownership of the fledgling business in 1916 and turned it into a successful enterprise before he sold his stake – at considerable profit – in 1923. Not a man to sit still for long, in 1927 he purchased a small boat yard at Hythe on Southampton Water and, keen to explore the technology of fast boats, he founded the British Power Boat Company.

Employing eminent boat designer Fred Cooper, Scott-Paine began to evolve the design of fast boat hulls. Together they began to develop a form of hard chine hull: boats with a traditional bow but sharp – almost 90-degree – angle between the sides and bottom of the hull towards the stern, making the boat nearly flat-bottomed at its rear. The design allowed the boat, when powered at speed, to lift up

out of the water and plane across the surface. These semi-planing hulls were both cheaper and easier to produce than the stepped hull design that had been successfully proven by Thornycroft three decades earlier.

Sport would again drive progress and the British Power Boat Company's boats were soon winning international competitions. In 1929 *Miss England* won the international racing event at the Miami Beach Yacht Club Regatta and in 1933 *Miss Britain III* achieved a speed of more than 100mph, a record for a single-engine boat that remained unbroken for 50 years. At the same time the company was developing a series of popular commercial boats that drew wide praise around Britain.

Scott-Paine was keen to see his boats in military service and it was not long before the company began to attract the attention of the Royal Air Force, who were looking for new, faster boats to serve their flying boats and operate as safety and rescue vessels. Championed by T.E. Lawrence, perhaps better known as Lawrence of Arabia, within a few years the company was building a variety of launches for different roles with the RAF's Marine Branch. The War Department also purchased boats for duties around their coastal firing ranges.

These early service boats revealed a need for suitable machinery and Scott-

Paine approached the engineering company Meadows to develop a marine version of their petrol engines. The new Power-Meadows engine was suitable for small boats, but something more substantial would be needed for larger, high-performance vessels. In 1932 he successfully converted a Napier Lion aircraft engine for marine use and the Napier company began an exclusive supply of the new Power-Napier Sea Lion engine to British Power Boat. Scott-Paine now had the engine he needed.

Although the Army and RAF were willing customers, the Admiralty were less keen. Eventually they accepted a number of improved launches for their larger warships and in 1935, after considerable persuasion by Scott-Paine and a handful of forward-thinking officers, they ordered two new torpedo boats. MTBs 01 and 02 – both of 60ft and powered by three Power-Napier Sea Lion engines – were commissioned on 30 June 1936. By the end of the year, a flotilla of six were in service.

The new MTBs shared some characteristics with the earlier CMBs. The torpedoes were once again carried at the stern of the boat, this time on rails suspended above the engines. Launching was achieved by opening hatches on the transom and applying an additional touch of speed to nudge the torpedoes into the water. The similarity to the CMB's launch method betrayed the complete lack of

development of MTBs between the wars – it was not until 1938 that staff at HMS *Vernon*, the Royal Navy torpedo and mining school, designed the familiar torpedo tubes that became an iconic facet of MTBs.

Scott-Paine didn't see the new craft as being limited only to torpedo boats. As the new MTBs were put through their paces, he conversed with the staff of HMS *Osprey* in Portland, advocating the use of the boats as fast submarine interceptors. The simple thinking was

ABOVE A 100-class RAF High Speed Launch during its trials on Southampton Water. During the Battle of Britain in 1940 these were the only high-speed rescue launches available to the RAF. *(Jeremy and Jeffrey Ridgway)*

LEFT MTB 01, the first Motor Torpedo Boat (MTB) to be commissioned into the Royal Navy. *(Author's Collection)*

Hubert Scott-Paine was born on 11 March 1890 in Shoreham-by-Sea. As he grew up he quickly developed an interest in engineering on wheels, at sea and later, in the air. In 1908, entrepreneur Noel Pemberton Billing moved to a property near Scott-Paine's home and the two families became friends. Scott-Paine was soon working on board the steam yachts that Pemberton Billing bought and sold around Europe.

BELOW **Hubert Scott-Paine.** *(Jeremy and Jeffrey Ridgway)*

In September 1913, Pemberton Billing purchased a simple 'aeroplane' and obtained his flying certificate. Together with Scott-Paine, new ideas for flying boats were sketched out and Pemberton Billing purchased a small yard at Woolston, across the River Itchen from Southampton, to build them. In November, Scott-Paine painted the name Supermarine on the wharf of the new yard and the following month he was appointed manager. A year later he purchased the majority stake in the firm.

In 1916, Pemberton Billing sold his remaining share to Scott-Paine who formally registered the firm as the Supermarine Aviation Company Limited. Over the next few years, he turned the fledgling business into a successful aircraft manufacturer and in 1920 employed Reginald Mitchell as a designer. In 1922, the Supermarine Seal II won the Schneider Trophy seaplane race, a precursor to the success that Supermarine would enjoy in the following nine years, when Mitchell's S5 and S6 seaplanes won the trophy for Britain outright.

Scott-Paine sold his share of Supermarine in 1923, acquiring for himself a small fortune. He began to experiment with boats and in 1927 he purchased the boat yard at Hythe and founded the British Power Boat Company.

Soon the yard was leading the way in boat design and with his designer Fred Cooper, British Power Boat built *Miss England*, used by Henry Segrave to set a new world speed record for single-engine motorboats in 1929. Although Cooper left acrimoniously later that year, Scott-Paine continued to develop boat designs with Cooper's assistant, Tommy Quelch. *Miss Britain I* followed and soon won racing events in the UK and the USA. When *Miss Britain III* was launched in 1933, it set a speed record for single-engine boats that remained unbroken for more than 50 years.

One of the contributors to *Miss Britain III* was George Selman. Born in 1896 in London, Selman studied engineering and naval architecture before working at the National Physical Laboratory in the early 1910s. He served in the Royal Navy during the First

World War but returned to ship design in the 1920s; by 1929 he was employed as a naval architect by the Manganese Bronze Company, designing propellers for giant ocean liners and small racing boats alike. Scott-Paine regarded Selman highly and in 1936 he offered him a job as chief designer. Selman's knowledge of boat design revolved around metal hulls, not wooden ones, but he studied his new medium carefully. When he undertook his first major design – that of PV 70 – he created a capable boat whose only flaw was perhaps the whaleback deck insisted on by Scott-Paine.

At the outbreak of the Second World War, Scott-Paine took the designs for PV 70 to the USA to lobby boat-builders there, leaving his design team free from interference. Selman designed most of British Power Boat's military boats during the war, including the famous 68ft RAF High Speed Launch (HSL) nicknamed the 'Hants and Dorset', owing to its wheelhouse's apparent similarity to a double-decker bus. He also designed several fast launches for Army service and even an airborne lifeboat. When British Power Boat closed in 1947 he continued to work in boat design for Lister Blackstone, designing engine installations and propulsion gear. He worked well into his 80s before he passed away in 1993 at the age of 97.

Scott-Paine spent the entirety of the war years in the USA, establishing his business interests in North America. In 1946 he suffered a stroke and did not return to the UK until 1951, when his racing boat *Miss Britain III* was formally presented to the National Maritime Museum. He passed away in 1954 at the age of 63.

Scott-Paine's forceful style upset many in the Admiralty through the years, earning him a number of enemies in high places and even prompting questions to be asked about his practices (unjustly) in parliament. It was perhaps for this reason that both he and Selman received far fewer accolades in post-war Britain than other boat designers (Peter Du Cane, for instance, was made a CBE). Perhaps most tellingly, when William Holt, Chief Constructor of the Naval Construction Department during the war, presented a paper on Coastal Forces design at a meeting of the Royal Institution of Naval Architects in 1947, no one from British Power Boat was invited to attend. This was only really rectified when Selman was awarded the Small Craft Group Medal by the institution in the year of his death – the only honour he ever received for his work.

BELOW **George Selman.** *(British Military Powerboat Trust – BMPT – Collection, via PNBPT)*

that a fast boat would be able to race towards a submarine it had spotted on the surface and drop depth charges before it had a chance to dive to safety. As a result, when the Admiralty ordered more MTBs in August 1936, one was specified to be suitable for anti-submarine work and another for minesweeping.

Nonetheless, the Admiralty had reservations about the size of Scott-Paine's boats. As they began to draw up policies for the future employment of these craft, they cast a critical eye over the six boats that now made up the 1st MTB Flotilla and noted that they would be too small for 21in torpedoes and not suitable for operations beyond coastal waters. What was needed was a larger boat, capable of handling rougher waters in the North Sea or the Mediterranean.

The 60ft MTB design had evolved from the original hard chine hull developed by Scott-Paine and Fred Cooper in the late 1920s. Cooper had by now left the company and worked for a rival firm based in Portsmouth – Vosper. Headed by ex-Royal Navy officer Peter Du Cane, Vosper had already been building small craft for the Admiralty for a number of years, but Du Cane was interested in producing something larger; he enquired about building an MTB. Officially, the Admiralty declined to place any orders, but Du Cane received some discreet advice from friends in the service and soon he had a list of specifications that the Royal Navy hoped to see in a future MTB. In 1936, Vosper began work on a private venture boat.

Work on the boat continued apace and by May 1937 it was ready to launch; 68ft long and powered by three Italian Isotta Fraschini engines, the boat could reach speeds of up to 43kts. A number of tests demonstrated its capabilities and the potential of the design to the Admiralty. Suitably impressed, they purchased her on 30 October and classified her as MTB 102, the 100-prefix indicating an experimental boat. In May 1938 the vessel was officially commissioned into the Royal Navy. Du Cane was elated, but disappointed to learn that the Admiralty had ordered another batch of Scott-Paine's 60ft MTBs, taking the total number up to 18.

Private Venture 70

Regardless of the supplier, the Admiralty were finally beginning to wake up to the role that small boats could play in the Royal Navy. In November 1937 they decided that future policy should be directed towards five types of boat:

- Fast anti-submarine boats
- Fast motor minesweepers
- 'Attack' MTBs, suitable for operations against enemy harbours
- 'Defence' MTBs suitable for home port defence
- 'Open Water' MTBs, suitable for seagoing operations.

Many officers in the Royal Navy remembered all too well the events of the First World War, when German U-boats had operated around Britain's coastline, sinking shipping within sight of the shore. Fortunately, Scott-Paine's experimental anti-submarine boat had just been completed and, even before it was commissioned, was undertaking trials in Portland.

The new boat was essentially an adaptation of his 60ft MTB design, powered by two engines instead of three as speed was not such an essential requirement. Instead of torpedoes, the boat was fitted with an ASDIC dome under the hull and an armament of depth charges. An early form of sonar, the ASDIC dome sent out a sound wave that would bounce off underwater objects and back to the dome. The sound wave could be sent in specific directions and the speed at which it returned would indicate range. Once an underwater target had been acquired, the boat could manoeuvre into a position to attack it with depth charges.

On 1 December 1937, Commander Cooper of the Royal Navy's Tactical Division sailed on the new 'Motor A/S Boat' during a series of tests and noted that its ASDIC performance 'exceeded all my expectations'. While hunting a Royal Navy submarine, the boat was able to detect its target on every trial run and the ASDIC even operated clearly at 30kts. Cooper commented that although 'there are many

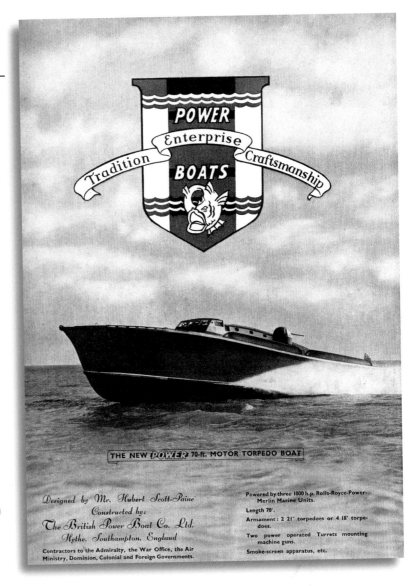

THE NEW *POWER* 70-ft. MOTOR TORPEDO BOAT

Designed by Mr. Hubert Scott-Paine
Constructed by:
The British Power Boat Co. Ltd.
Hythe, Southampton, England
Contractors to the Admiralty, the War Office, the Air Ministry, Dominion, Colonial and Foreign Governments.

Powered by three 1000 h.p. Rolls-Royce-Power-Merlin Marine Units.
Length 70'.
Armament : 2 21" torpedoes or 4 18" torpedoes.
Two power operated Turrets mounting machine guns.
Smoke-screen apparatus, etc.

problems to be considered and solved before Motor A/S Boats can be proved efficient A/S craft, the early results show distinct promise'. The staff of HMS *Osprey* were even more enthusiastic and later that month the Admiralty ordered that six new 60ft boats be included in the 1938 building programme.

ABOVE AND BELOW

British Power Boat's PV 70, the hull of which became the basis for all their subsequent designs. *(Jeremy and Jeffrey Ridgway)*

Despite the Admiralty's enthusiasm for this type of boat, Scott-Paine had already anticipated that the Royal Navy would soon require something larger. Vosper's private venture represented a threat to his monopoly on small Royal Navy craft, so he would need to design something quickly. Fortunately, he had recently hired a new chief designer, George Selman, who would help him achieve this.

Scott-Paine knew that he could not simply stretch his existing 60ft hull and instead envisaged a new design of a 70ft boat. Under Selman's instruction, design work on the new boat had proceeded through 1937 and construction began in utmost secrecy in May 1938. Six months later, on 6 November the new boat, known as PV 70, was launched.

The new boat was 70ft long with a 20ft-wide beam towards the bow. The frames used laminated beams in the places of greatest stress and the hull was planked in double diagonal planking throughout. Scott-Paine had managed to broker a deal with Rolls-Royce to develop a marine version of the Merlin engine, and three of these would provide the power. Perhaps its most distinctive feature was the deck: the high bow curved down into a reverse sheer aft of the wheelhouse. The design had been an experimental model that Selman discounted, but Scott-Paine saw the shape as an asset to his company. Selman knew it weakened the hull significantly and would eventually be proved right, but Scott-Paine was unmoved. The classic hull form was certainly distinctive, though: it was so iconic that the British Power Boat High Speed Launches that used the same hull form became the most famous of all rescue boats in RAF service (even though only 69 were ever built), acquiring the nickname 'whalebacks'.

PV 70 was undoubtedly a masterpiece of marine engineering and performed well in trials for both the Royal Navy and foreign governments. The Admiralty were impressed, but in 1939 ultimately decided to focus on the Vosper designs for their future MTBs. Scott-Paine and Selman were crushed – they knew that not only was their design very likely superior to MTB 102, but that they had the yard and facilities to mass-produce the boat quickly. The Admiralty did agree to change the order for MA/SB 6, the final MA/SB of their previous order, to be built as a 70ft boat using the new hull design, although this represented little recompense.

This reluctant interest in small fast boats shown by the Admiralty was not shared by every nation. In the wake of the First World War

BELOW Despite PV 70's performance, the Admiralty chose to base their future MTBs on Vosper's design. Vosper 70ft MTBs became one of the more iconic representations of Coastal Forces.
(Peter Scott)

the CMB's success had piqued the interest
of other nations: Thornycroft had continued
to manufacture the boats for export to several
navies, including the French, Dutch, Finnish,
Swedish, US, Japanese and Chinese. When
Selman experimented with a shorter hull version
of PV 70, reducing the length to 63ft, both boats
appealed to foreign navies. In March 1939 the
Dutch government ordered a 70ft boat, followed
by the French government who ordered 18 of
the 70ft boats in the summer. The Swedish
government ordered two of the 63ft boats and
the Norwegians ordered four. All were to be
completed as MTBs.

In September 1939, Scott-Paine took one
of the PV 70 boats to the USA, where he
found enthusiastic interest from boatbuilder
Elco in Bayonne, New Jersey. The boat was
commissioned as PT 9 and became the
basis of Elco's early PT boats. Then, as war
descended on Europe, he approached the
engineering firm Packard. Their M-2500
engine, developed experimentally for PT
boats, appeared an ideal type to be further
adapted for use in his boats and, over the
following two months, arrangements were
made to modify the design using Scott-Paine's
experience of marinising the Rolls-Royce
Merlin. In December, he placed an order for

100 of the new 4M-2500 engines to supply
the Elco boats being built to his designs and
secured the rights for distribution of the engine
throughout the British Empire.

War

When Britain declared war on
3 September 1939, there were pitifully
few fast motorboats in service. More were
hastily ordered the next day as part of the
Emergency War Programme, including boats
from Vosper, Thornycroft, J. Samuel White and a
further 33 70ft MA/SBs from British Power Boat.

The existing flotilla of British Power Boat
MA/SBs, however, remained somewhat
dormant. In principle the MA/SB had seemed
a sensible concept, but in practice, things
were very different. The five 60ft boats were
formed into the 1st MA/SB Flotilla and based
at Portland at the outbreak of the war. There
was, however, little for them to do: contrary
to the experience of the First World War,
Germany did not send masses of U-boats into
the Channel and the small boats spent most of
their time patrolling Britain's coast.

Meanwhile, the 1st MTB Flotilla (60ft British
Power Boat MTBs) was recalled from the
Mediterranean. After a difficult journey through

the canals of France, in January 1940 those vessels that were sufficiently serviceable were sent to Felixstowe to be joined by the recently completed Vosper and Thornycroft boats.

In December 1939, MA/SB 6, the experimental 70ft boat, was accepted into service, quickly followed by three more 70ft boats completed by the spring of 1940. The British government was also beginning to requisition boats that were completing for foreign governments. Boats that had not yet been sent to France, Sweden and Norway were claimed by the British government who redesignated them as MA/SBs.

In April, MA/SBs 2 and 3 were shipped to the Mediterranean where, for a year, they were the only two fast boats of the Royal Navy operating in the region. MA/SB 3 was pressed into service as an emergency minesweeper, running at high speed across mines in the hope of detonating them in the wake. The principle was as dangerous as it sounds, and MA/SB 3's hull was damaged beyond repair when a mine detonated under it in February 1941. She was paid off shortly after, followed by MA/SB 2 in 1942. Along with the 1st MTB Flotilla, which had long since departed in 1939, these were the only other British Power Boats to see Royal Navy service in the Mediterranean in the war.

At the end of May 1940, MA/SBs 6 and 7 were despatched to Dunkirk to assist with the evacuation of the British Expeditionary Force. They were quickly joined by MA/SB 10, which was rushed into service before there was even time to paint her hull. The boats shuttled soldiers from the beaches to bigger ships offshore and returned 64 men direct to England. MA/SB 6 even had the honour of carrying Lord Gort, the Commander-in-Chief of the British Expeditionary Force in France, back to Dover.

Meanwhile, Selman had been further developing his 63ft whaleback design. The 70ft boats, equipped with three Power-Napier Sea Lion engines, made a great deal of noise and created significant interference with the ASDIC equipment. An experimental 63ft boat being built for South Africa was used for tests in June 1940 and it was found that the new boat performed better than the 70ft design with three engines. After discussions between the Admiralty and British Power Boat, it was decided to switch the production of the Emergency War Programme order for 33 70ft boats to the 63ft design, starting with MA/SB 22. The boats being built for France but requisitioned by Britain would continue to be completed as 70ft boats.

At last, however, the Admiralty were realising

the importance of a fleet of small, fast craft and the Navy's 'little ships' grew in number. More boats were coming into service to operate on the east coast and in the Channel, where a growing threat was emerging.

Schnellboote

In Germany the success of the small torpedo boat had been especially noted. The Imperial German Navy had experimented with small torpedo-carrying hydroplanes in the First World War – although designed primarily as defensive boats they had scored some success, sinking a Russian minelayer in the Baltic in 1917. As early as 1925, the post-war Reichsmarine began to experiment with fast military boats. Hamstrung by the requirements of the Treaty of Versailles – which limited the German Navy to six battleships, six cruisers and twelve destroyers – the fast motorboat offered an alternative avenue for experimentation and training. Realising that such boats might be considered torpedo boats by Britain, France and the USA, their development was kept secret – not least because torpedo boats were very much in the mind of the designers.

Numerous hull and propulsion designs were trialled over the following years and in 1929

the firm of Lürssen, based in Bremen, was contracted to supply a fast motorboat direct to the Reichsmarine. Delivered in 1930, the boat was officially classified as *Schnellboot* S 1 in 1932. It was quickly followed by four more.

The new *Schnellboote* were revolutionary military fast boats. Although they used a traditional round bilge hull, they could achieve speeds of 34kts and were far more stable in rough seas than planing hulls. S 6 brought further improvements in the form of a diesel engine that substantially increased the efficiency and range of the boats and the following series – S 7 to S 13 – were commissioned between 1934 and 1935. Ostensibly unarmed, they were designed to fit two torpedo tubes on the bow, forward of the bridge, with the intention that when the political situation allowed, torpedo tubes would be fitted to all of them. Even without torpedoes, the boats themselves provided a valuable platform for training and tactical development in manoeuvres in the Baltic. Thus, when Germany went to war with Poland on 1 September 1939, it did so with two well-trained flotillas of S-boats.

With the fall of France, the Kriegsmarine was free to operate from ports all along the North Sea and Channel coasts, a situation that perfectly suited their flotillas of S-boats. It didn't

ABOVE The recall of the 1st Flotilla of 60ft British Power Boats provided the Royal Navy with some badly needed MTBs for home waters. Outwardly, these boats were almost identical to the 60ft MA/SBs.
(Author's Collection)

BELOW An early S-boat – most likely an S 14 class – on builder's trials before the war. Prior to the S 26 class, S-boats had their torpedo tubes mounted on top of the foredeck, from where they could be removed to hide the boat's true purpose. Later models incorporated the tubes directly into the hull, beneath a raised foredeck. *(Naval History and Heritage Command, NH43636)*

take them long to exploit it. They had already had success at Dunkirk, with boats of both flotillas intercepting and torpedoing vessels off the beaches, including the destroyer HMS *Wakeful*. Packed with British infantry as she sailed for Dover, her sinking claimed the lives of more than 700 men. Once the European coast was secure, the 1st Flotilla moved to Cherbourg and the 2nd to Ostend. Now the coastal convoys along England's southern and eastern coasts were vulnerable and the S-boats took full advantage.

On the night of 4 July, the 1st Flotilla made their first kills when four boats intercepted convoy OA 178, sinking one large merchant ship and damaging two more. Thereafter regular sorties found easy targets sailing singly or in convoys at night. On the east coast, the 2nd Flotilla made their first kill on 8 July and

then conducted regular minelaying operations along the convoy routes. Harried by the Luftwaffe during the day and by S-boats at night, Britain's convoys began to suffer.

This was a situation that Britain hadn't prepared for – the country was critically short of equipment needed to fight across the Channel – heavy bombers, Air-Sea Rescue facilities and landing craft – and now, rather than submarines prowling the coast, the Kriegsmarine was deploying surface vessels to attack its coastal convoys. Escort destroyers and corvettes struggled to engage these small, fast-moving boats with their conventional armament and the growing fleet of MTBs and MA/SBs were similarly ill equipped: torpedoes were no use against small, fast boats and the machine guns fitted to the boats were too light in calibre to take on the more heavily

armed enemy. What was needed was a fast boat equipped with quick-firing, heavy-calibre machine guns and cannon.

It did not take the Admiralty long to see the solution. While the MTBs launching from boat yards on a regular basis had a useful function – engaging enemy coastal convoys off France, Belgium and the Netherlands – the growing fleet of MA/SBs had little purpose. The Kriegsmarine's U-boats were operating from the western coast of France, sailing direct into the ocean to attack Atlantic convoys, well beyond the reach of small 70ft boats. But perhaps, with some small modifications, the MA/SBs could serve as gun boats to counter the S-boat threat.

New boats for a new threat

Meanwhile, the 2nd and 3rd MA/SB Flotillas had formed at Portland, although still no one really knew how best to employ them. The threat from U-boats was negligible and on 12 August an instruction was sent to British Power Boat that ASDIC sets would no longer need to be installed in any of the boats requisitioned from foreign navies (although for a short while they continued to be installed on the boats of the Emergency War Programme order).

The 3rd Flotilla was created from a mix of 63ft and 70ft boats that had originally been destined for France and Scandinavia. With no other function, the flotilla began a myriad of different tasks, including racing across mines dropped by enemy aircraft in Plymouth Harbour and, more conventionally, anti-S-boat patrols in the Channel. Their most significant contribution in those early months came on the night of 10/11 October, providing escort duties when HMS *Revenge* bombarded Cherbourg.

It was clear that the boats were more useful fighting an enemy on the surface and thoughts turned to how best to equip them in an anti-S-boat role. ASDIC sets and most of the depth charges were removed, freeing up weight and space for guns. The new armament comprised twin Vickers machine-gun turrets and, where available, antiquated artillery pieces such as the Rolls-Royce 2-pounder.

Originally the boats had been equipped with two Power-Napier Sea Lion engines that produced a top speed of only 23kts on a fully laden boat, insufficient for most types of surface action. Fortunately, the 18 boats meant for France (which had been requisitioned as MA/SBs 50 to 67) had been ordered as more powerful MTBs with three marinised Rolls-Royce Merlin engines. Although they would be the only boats that were equipped with these engines (they were in short supply and the Air Ministry quickly secured all future Rolls-

ABOVE **70ft MA/SB 16, probably after her conversion to an MGB, as she is not equipped with depth charges.**
(Peter Scott)

Royce output for their aircraft), they provided the Royal Navy with the first boats that were powerful enough to serve as gun boats.

However, the new role placed considerable stress on the MA/SBs' hulls. Of particular concern was the stress caused by high-speed manoeuvring in rough seas. The addition of heavier weaponry also affected the boats' frames and quickly caused hull failures. Nonetheless, in November 1940 the Admiralty placed an order for 24 more MA/SBs to build their flotillas. At the time, the Royal Navy needed boats and if British Power Boat had capacity, they should obtain them – even if they weren't the most suitable. Aware of the operational problems the existing boats were having, in that same month Vice Admiral Francis Tower, Director of Naval Equipment, contacted British Power Boat to discuss the potential of a purpose-built gun boat.

By now Scott-Paine resided in North America, looking after his interests there and in the newly founded Canadian Power Boat Company, which he hoped would receive more orders for MTBs from Britain. In his absence, Tower approached Selman to discuss a new boat. Scott-Paine was concerned that Selman would not be able to produce a design without his own input, but accepted that his distance from the company's Hythe factory would make his participation impossible. Design work on the new boats began in December 1940 and Selman's team worked night and day perfecting the hull, armaments and machinery and conducting tank tests.

Selman's design was for a 71ft 6in (21.8m) long boat. The hard chine semi-planing hull was essentially the same as that of the earlier 70ft MA/SBs, but slightly longer and significantly stronger. Knowing that the boats in service were already suffering frame damage and that the gunwales were being reinforced with extra timber to prevent the boat fracturing, Selman did away with the reverse sheer 'whaleback' deck, replacing it with a hog sheer deck to better distribute stress over the length of the boat. The hull was surfaced with double diagonal planking with triple planking below the chine.

The boat would be powered by three of the Packard 4M-2500 marine engines, each producing 1,200hp. Some 2,733 gallons of fuel situated below the chart room allowed for a range of 550nm at 20kts or 600nm at 15kts, with a maximum speed of 42 or 43kts when the boat was fully laden. Forward of the fuel tanks were a small galley and officers' cabin with the crew mess forward.

To wholly fulfil its role as a gun boat, Selman intended to mount a 40mm 2-pounder pom-pom gun forward of the wheelhouse and a twin 20mm Oerlikon gun aft, both in powered turrets. Four Lewis guns in twin hand-operated mountings on either side of the bridge would provide close defence, a Holman Projector at the stern would offer some anti-aircraft

defence, while two depth charges and a star shell gun completed the armament.

Selman and his team had the designs for their new boat – designated Mk V – ready by February 1941 and that month he met Tower and William Holt, Chief Constructor of the Naval Construction Department, at a conference in Bath. Holt was unimpressed – he did not think the boat would be able to perform in anything worse than a force 2 or 3 sea and was inclined to reject the design. However, Admiral Tower quickly intervened and stated that this was the boat he wanted and therefore the design that would be built. The Admiralty updated their November order to utilise the new design, although the following month they reduced it from 24 boats to a single flotilla of 8.

Things were changing at a higher level as well. In November 1940, Coastal Forces was officially established as a division of the Royal Navy under its own Flag Officer – Rear Admiral Piers Kekewich. Appointed as his staff officer was Captain Augustus Agar who, 21 years earlier, had sunk the *Oleg* in his CMB and now brought vital experience to the new command. The following January a new designation for all boats primarily equipped with guns was formalised. Henceforth they would be known as Motor Gun Boats.

BELOW Early gun boats of the 2nd MGB Flotilla. All have been fitted with gun turrets on either side of the bridge. *(Peter Scott)*

Chapter Two

Building an MGB

By the mid-1900s, small boat-building had evolved into an industry founded on solid engineering principles. Precision techniques ensured that boats conformed accurately to plans and drawings, to guarantee they would work as efficiently as their design intended. By 1942, the Admiralty too had developed procedures to ensure that Coastal Forces crews were as well trained as possible.

OPPOSITE **At work on the keel of a British Power Boat hull. Counter-intuitively, British Power Boat vessels began life upside down.** *(Coastal Forces Heritage Trust – CFHT – Collection)*

RIGHT The jig laid out on the workshop floor at Elco's yard in the United States, ready to commence construction of a Patrol Torpedo (PT) boat. Early Elco PT boats were built to the same design as PV 70 and in an almost identical fashion. *(US Navy)*

Constructing a hull

The Admiralty records for MGB 81 state that she was laid down on 16 December 1941. The phrase 'laid down' originates from the traditional start of a ship's construction, when the keel is laid out in a yard. In shipbuilding the keel is the core part of the hull and all other elements of a ship's structure are built around it. At British Power Boat, as at some other small boatbuilders around the world, the hulls of the boats were built upside down. The boat's life began with the construction of a jig on the workshop floor, into which the topside beams of the main hull frames were set. Once the frames were in place, the keel was laid on top and set into the lower parts of each frame.

The British Power Boat Mk V Motor Gun Boat had 62 frames, including the transom (the flat stern of the boat). The frames were sawn, meaning that separate lengths of wood were joined to complete the frame's overall shape, with a minimum of bending of each beam. A typical hard chine hull frame consisted of five timber beams – the topside (or deck) beams, the two bottom (or floor) beams and the side beams. The separate beams were joined to one another using plywood gussets – brackets that were glued and screwed to the lengths of wood being joined. Six of the frames were completed as timber watertight bulkheads, adding rigidity to the hull and a necessary layer of damage control to the boat's interior. To further reinforce the bow deck where the 2-pounder gun was fitted, Selman added two longitudinal bulkheads, effectively placing two supporting walls beneath the gun mount.

Mahogany was the preferred wood for

RIGHT A typical frame. There are five main parts – at the top the topside beam, the side beams and two bottom beams. Plywood gussets connect the sides to the bottom beams. *(US Navy)*

frames, owing to its light weight, low rate of shrinkage and its resistance to rot, although other hardwoods such as oak were suitable substitutes. Laminated beams were often used in the areas of most stress on the hull, usually on the bottom beams which would be highly stressed as a boat planed.

Normally separate jigs would be required for each of a hull's frames so that each unique shape could be accurately formed – for a Mk V boat this would have required 62 separate jigs! At British Power Boat this had been simplified by the creation of a single, adjustable jig. A metal plate larger than the boat's largest frame served as the base of the jig, and metal guides were made for each possible position of the keel, gunwales and chine. Sawn timbers or laminated beams were inserted into the jig and the guides placed in the necessary positions for that frame. The system made it possible to form frames of different sizes with minimal adjustment of the jig and was accurate and efficient, with frames being produced quicker than they were being put into boats.

The keel was typically laminated wood. Laminated timber beams were created by

DOUBLE DIAGONAL PLANKING

For centuries, most wooden boat hulls were constructed with carvel- or clinker-built planking – both designs using long timbers laid end to end along the length of the boat. In 1826, William Johns, master boatbuilder at Plymouth Dockyard, designed a new hull-planking method. Rather than using timbers along the length of the hull, his method involved laying short planks aligned diagonally (or semi-vertically) from top to bottom. A second layer of diagonal planking was then fitted on top, laying at opposite angles to the first.

The design proved effective: as well as being a more efficient method of manufacturing small boat hulls, using shorter lengths of wood and requiring fewer tools, the opposing planks added extra rigidity to the hull when complete. In 1831, Lieutenant Robert FitzRoy requested that two boats 'built on Mr Johns' principle of Diagonal planking' be constructed for his ship HMS *Beagle*, which subsequently carried Charles Darwin to the Galapagos Islands. Johns was awarded £300 for his invention in 1840.

By the 1940s, double diagonal planking was a popular and effective method of motorboat hull construction. Unfortunately, though, it can have a detrimental effect on the hull of boats over time: the cloth sandwiched between the layers eventually ceases to work effectively as a waterproof membrane and in older boats can act as a wick, transporting damp across the hull when water penetrates the outer layer.

LEFT The stern of 70ft MGB 60 or 61, photographed in 1999. The plain timbers are the inner diagonal planks and the blue ones are the outer skin, running across the inner layer at 90 degrees. *(Philip Simons)*

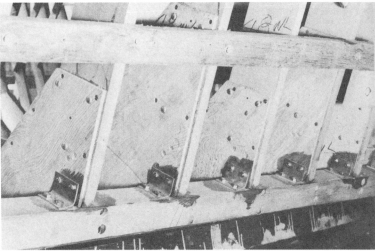

between the deck and the chine. The chines were solid wood timbers (steam-bent to allow them to curve sufficiently around the shape of the hull) that ran along the length of the outside of the vessel at the join between the side and bottom beams of the frames.

At the bottom of the hull, Selman provided extra strength with longitudinal girders. At the stern, four thick-set timbers ran from the transom to the fuel tanks and doubled as engine supports. Forward, four longitudinal timber girders continued to the bow. Webs – small timber panels – were glued and braced between the girders athwartships (from port to starboard) at each frame. The result was a grid across the lower hull that increased its rigidity and resistance to longitudinal stresses.

With the skeleton of the hull completed, the next element was the skin. Scott-Paine had experimented with diagonal planking in his early boat designs and moving on to double diagonal hulls was a natural next step. The 60ft torpedo boats used double diagonal planking below the chine, with single diagonal planks on the sides of the hull, but Selman extended the double diagonal across the entire hull on PV 70, the two layers separated by a layer of calico fabric soaked in linseed oil or white lead paste, which served as a waterproof membrane. For the new gun boats, he strengthened the hull further by using triple diagonal planking below the chine.

Once the hull was completed, the boat could be rotated using an overhead crane. Additional cambered deck beams were laid across the top of the hull athwartships, running parallel to the topside beams of the frames, while deck stringers ran longitudinally the length of the hull. Two layers of plywood decking, like the hull separated by fabric soaked in linseed oil or white lead, completed the exterior decks.

The deck superstructure on the Mk V gun boat was relatively straightforward. The bridge, chartroom, radio room, RDF (range and direction finding) office and the mount for the rear gun position were all contained within a single structure that was collectively called the wheelhouse on the boat drawings, but was also known as the coach roof. The long wheelhouse borrowed somewhat from the design first seen in PV 70, but was set further back to allow more room at the bow for the 2-pounder.

building up several layers (or laminations) of thin wood, bound together with glue or bolts. By joining numerous layers with parallel grains, it was possible to create substantial timbers, relatively much stronger than similarly sized beams of solid wood. An additional benefit was that the beam could be completed with a moulded curve (thin layers are easier to curve over their length than a solid section of wood). The keel was usually completed in two parts – the largely straight bottom part and the upward-curving bow section. The two were joined using a scarf joint and the completed piece lowered on to the upside-down frames.

The next elements to be added to the hull were the longitudinal supports. At deck level, sheer clamps ran along the joins between the gussets and topside beams of each frame, providing rigidity to the sheer (or curve) of the upper deck, while stringers ran along the sides

TOP LEFT Timber girders of box beam construction running along the bottom beams of a boat's frames. *(US Navy)*

TOP RIGHT The forward mess with decking removed. The keel can be seen at the bottom of the boat. Parallel to it are the four longitudinal beams, while running athwartships are the numerous webs. *(PNBPT)*

CENTRE The first layer of diagonal planking is attached to the bottom of the hull. *(US Navy)*

LEFT Marine glue is used to attach the fabric to the inner layer of diagonal planking. Once this is attached, the second layer can be laid over it. A familiar whaleback hull can be seen in the background. *(US Navy)*

RIGHT Once the hull is complete, the boat can be rotated using overhead cranes. *(US Navy)*

BELOW A Canadian Power Boat worker assembling the gun turret on a 70ft boat. Like all Coastal Forces boats, the wheelhouse was made of timber and only the bridge had any armour plate on the Mk V and Mk VI boats. *(Library and Archives Canada/PA-132175)*

BELOW Canadian Power Boat workers deck the bow of a 70ft boat. *(Library and Archives Canada/PA-132179)*

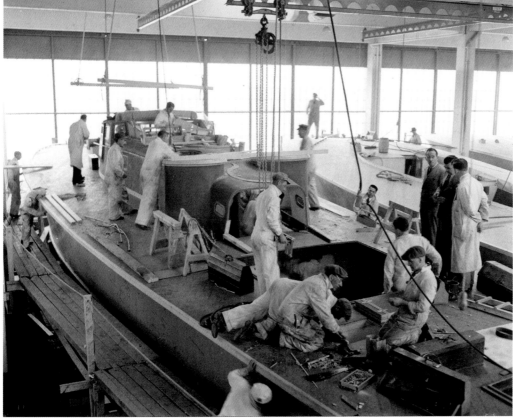

Canadian Power Boat workers attach the wheelhouse superstructure to the deck of a 70ft boat. *(Library and Archives Canada/PA-132180)*

LEFT Canadian Power Boat workers complete the engine room hatch on a 70ft boat. *(Library and Archives Canada/ PA-132181)*

THE BRITISH POWER BOAT COMPANY

Hythe is not an ideal place to build boats, primarily on account of the large mud banks that project from the shore on the west side of Southampton Water. Nonetheless, boats have been built at the waterfront settlement since the 16th century and, in the early 18th century, a yard was established on the site that would eventually become British Power Boat.

Owned by a local shipbuilding family, during the Napoleonic Wars this small yard expanded with the construction of several small warships for the Royal Navy.

Boatbuilding became a minor industry at Hythe after the war and it was not until 1884 that the yard prospered again, this time when the British Yacht Club opened a

new headquarters next door. To protect their members' boats, the club built two moles to create a small harbour and, in 1922, the yard and harbour were both acquired by Robert Kemp who transformed them into a modern boat yard with high-class facilities for maintaining luxury yachts.

On 30 September 1927, Scott-Paine bought the yard at auction and founded the British Power Boat Company. Over the following 12 years before war broke out, he moulded the company into an efficient boatbuilding firm that operated to standards way ahead of their time. Disaster had struck in 1931 when a fire destroyed almost the entire boat yard, but it provided the opportunity to build a modern facility with up-to-date tools and equipment. The yard was laid out like a production line, with incoming timber going straight

The British Power Boat yard in 1940, photographed by a Luftwaffe reconnaissance aircraft. The company branding on the roofs has been replaced with camouflaged paint. *(Luftwaffe aerial photograph, GX10338 SG, The National Archives at College Park, College Park, MD)*

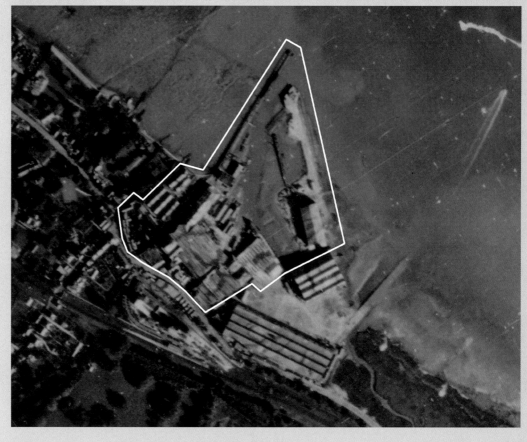

from the stores to the sawmill next door and then directly to the workshops. The workshops themselves were always swept and kept immaculately tidy – an automatic expectation in workplaces today, but very much an innovation at the time. By 1939, British Power Boat operated less like a typical boat yard and more like a factory.

With so many men joining the services during the war, women were employed in large numbers at British Power Boat. Nearby Marchwood House was purchased and turned into a training centre for women workers, who underwent a two-month training course before moving into the workshops at Hythe. The wartime working conditions for the staff at British Power Boat could be arduous. To keep the yard running constantly the 24-hour day was split into two shifts, with staff typically working 10 hours and occasionally being asked to run over to get boats finished. Nor was this work solely in a boat shed – launched vessels moored in the harbour needed to be fitted out, a task that was done in all seasons and all weathers. Only air raids tended to stop work.

But the staff at British Power Boat enjoyed many benefits, including good rates of pay, welfare arrangements, modern canteen facilities and incentive schemes for apprentice boatbuilders. As apprentices reached various grades in their work, they were awarded vouchers to exchange for tools. By the end of the apprenticeships, they would have a complete tool-box. The BBC radio show *Music While You Work* was broadcast through the factory's tannoy and ENSA concerts were frequent. One of the employees, Harry Gigg, recalled that 'another of Scotty's great gestures (in 1937) was to give us paid holiday. This was unbelievable and had never been known before. Staff had paid holidays but never anywhere did those who worked by the clock get anything.'[1]

The Hythe yard expanded significantly in the war and a secondary yard was opened at Poole. Small boats were needed in all three arms of service and in total British Power

ABOVE **A wartime poster for Thornycroft. The employment of women in a traditionally male-led industry during the war was something that boatbuilders celebrated.** (Motor Boat and Yachting *magazine, 1943*)

Boat built more than 1,000 boats of all sizes that served in Coastal Forces, RAF Air-Sea Rescue and the Royal Army Service Corps. The inevitable downturn in orders in 1945 meant that it was uneconomical to run in peacetime. British Power Boat wound down in 1946 and finally closed in 1947. The satellite facility at Poole was closed and although Scott-Paine considered establishing a new yard at Marchwood, this too was sold off the following year.

1   Geoff Smith, 1991, p. 8.

ABOVE **Canadian Power Boat workers tune a Packard engine before it is installed into the boat.** *(Library and Archives Canada/PA-132178)*

BELOW **After servicing in the field, a Packard engine is lowered into the engine room of Vosper MTB 411.** *(Robert Westwood Collection, via PNBPT)*

Fitting machinery

At this stage, machinery and interior fittings could be installed. Working with Scott-Paine and incorporating developments made with the marinisation of the Rolls-Royce engine, Packard had developed the 4M-2500 marine petrol engine. The finished engine was a supercharged V12 four-stroke engine rated at 1,200hp at 2,400rpm and 1,350hp at 2,500rpm. Scott-Paine's initial order for 100 units was enough to put the engine into mass production and motivated him to lobby the Admiralty to secure this source of engines for boats being built in the UK. With Rolls-Royce engines and the pre-war Italian Isotta Fraschini engines no longer available to boatbuilders, the Packard represented Britain's best hope of obtaining suitably powerful engines for their fleet of MTBs and MGBs. In June 1940 the British Purchasing Commission placed their first order and by the end of the war, some 4,686 4M-2500 Packard engines had been purchased or sent to Britain under Lend-Lease.

The central engine sat between the

bulkhead at frame 42 and frame 48, powering a direct shaft. The port and starboard engine sat behind, between frames 46 and 52, but faced backwards and powered their propeller shafts with vee drives. Each was connected to its gearbox ahead of it by a short Cardan shaft and the main shaft ran underneath it towards the stern. Behind these in the tiller flat, the exhausts fed out through the transom.

Between the bulkheads at frames 26 and 42 were the five petrol tanks that held 2,600 gallons of fuel between them. Forward of these was the crew space, with separate sections divided by the bulkheads. A small wardroom was provided for the officers and further forward a galley and the crew mess deck at the bow. Creature comforts came in the form of classic Baby Blake marine toilets.

Readying for launch

As the boat neared completion, the Admiralty would frequently assign officers to 'stand by' the vessel, often giving more experienced officers a chance to request minor modifications to the layout of the bridge or cabins. At the yard they met Lieutenant Eric Hill who represented the Admiralty at British Power Boat and obtained all the necessary equipment each boat would need, from navigation equipment to pots of paint. As final completion approached, the rest of the ship's crew would arrive, ready to begin work as soon as she was in the water.

Once the vessel was structurally complete, she was ready for launch. The frequency with which boats were produced at the yard meant that launch ceremonies could not always be grand affairs attended by dignitaries and the press. Small wonder, given that more than 550 boats slid down British Power Boat's slips in Hythe during the Second World War, meaning a boat was launched on average every four

ABOVE MGB 116 at her launch ceremony on 18 February 1943. *(IWM A14597)*

BELOW Mk VI MTB 459 running on the British Power Boat measured mile on Southampton Water. The chapel tower at the Royal Victoria Hospital at Netley can just be made out in the background. *(BMPT Collection, via PNBPT)*

days. Nonetheless, when MGB 116 was launched in February 1943, the ceremony was overseen by Vice Admiral Sir James Pipon, the Flag Officer in Charge at Southampton. The flag-decked boat was launched down the slipway by one of the female workers to the cheers of a considerable assembled crowd.

Large warships were typically launched once the hull and superstructure were complete and then taken to a dockyard to be fitted out with armaments and equipment. Coastal Forces craft could be completed almost entirely in the yard and this was sometimes the case, although weapons and highly secretive equipment such as the RDF sets might instead be added at a naval base.

Once in the water, the new boat underwent tests and trials to fine-tune the engines, swing the compass and calibrate her weapons. After the boat was ready, she underwent her Admiralty acceptance trials, a four-hour test in the Solent and along Southampton Water's measured mile. On the successful conclusion

of the test, the boat was formally accepted into the Royal Navy.

Usually a few days later, the boat was formally commissioned. Lieutenant Commander Anthony Law, senior officer of the 29th (Canadian) MTB Flotilla, recalled that 'all day loads of ammunition and stores were brought aboard – it was like Christmas with all the lovely new equipment – and Lieutenant Hill assisted in his usual role of Santa Claus, while differing departments of BP were making "rabbits" (gifts for the boats) for us'.[2] Quite often commissioning ceremonies were a better opportunity to celebrate than the launch and, in between loading stores and

2   Law, 1989, p. 24.

RIGHT AND BELOW A list of fixtures incorporated into Mk VI boat MTB 484 during her fitting-out at British Power Boat in 1945. *(BMPT Collection, via PNBPT)*

D.—6c. (Steam or Motor Boat).   (Revised—Aug., 1937)

_____ Yard,

_____, 19   .

STEAM OR MOTOR BOAT ATTACHED to H.M.S._____

*LIST OF FIXTURES in charge of the

SHIPWRIGHT OFFICER

(a) Detailed List of the Fixtures supplied by _The British Power Co. Ltd. Hythe_

under Contract, dated _____ Reg. No. of Invoice _____

FOR

Steam or Motor _Torpedo_ Boat   No. ____ feet.

Warship Production Superintendent.

(a) For use as enclosure to D.6.

WE hereby Certify that the Fixtures, &c., shown herein are on board.

Navigating Officer.   Manager, Constructive Department.

For and on behalf of THE BRITISH POWER BOAT CO. LTD.

Assistant Constructor or Foreman of the Yard.

Shipwright Officer.

The Officer to whom the Fixtures, &c., are chargeable has been duly supplied with a List of the articles.

Superintending Naval Store Officer.

* A copy is to be forwarded to the Admiralty on delivery of the boat from Contractor's works as soon as the fixtures can be certified as placed on board and subsequently on any occasion when the list is closed and new lists are raised by the Dockyard.
Note.—Column 3 of this form is to be filled in for all items, "Nil" being inserted where necessary.

Sta./86/37.

DESCRIPTION	Denomination of Quantity	Torpedo Boat No. 484 Length 71'6" Quantity	Fixtures found on paying off	For use of Yard Officers	
				Left on Board	Returned to Store
Awning, Sun, canvas, complete with spreaders, covers, &c.	Set	Nil			
Awnings, boat, rain		Nil			
Back board, when portable {with hinged panel} {without}	No.				
Balers, Self		5			
Ballast, lead or iron	Tons	Nil			
Bars, depression, portable	No.	Nil			
Bearers, over stern sheets, and cover		Nil			
Beckets for rifles		4			
Belaying pins					
Bollards		Nil			
Canopies, canvas, with rods, straps, sliding pieces, tenons, clamps, life-lines, &c., complete		1			
Casing around upper or lower half of flywheel		Nil			
Chafing plates on rubbers		Nil			
Chain locker or box, with cable clench		1			
" pipe, metal		Nil			
Cleats, metal, Fender		Nil			
" for rig fittings		Nil			
Coamings, metal, portable		Nil			
Covers, metal, of sorts		1			
" to manholes, &c., portable		Nil			
" for motor, complete		Nil			
" canvas, for awnings		Nil			
" " boats		Nil			
" " engine,		3			
" " sails		Nil			
Cowls, ventilating					
Cradles (wood), for barricoes		Nil			
Curtains					

‡ Here insert the Description, Length, and Number of Boat in which the articles are fitted

DESCRIPTION	Denomination of Quantity	Torpedo Boat No. 484 Length 71'6" Quantity	Fixtures found on paying off	For use of Yard Officers	
				Left on Board	Returned to Store
Cushions in canvas covers	No.	6			
" leather covers	"	5			
" overcases for	"	44			
Deck filler cap to petrol tank	"	2			
Deck plates	"	4			
Dodger, canvas, with supports (for helmsman's shelter)	"	1			
Doors, wood (including hinged covers and fronts to lockers)	"	48			
Doors, W.T.	"	5			
Dolphins	"	Nil			
Eye-bolts, for canopy lifelines, &c.	"	Nil			
Elevators, metal	"	Nil			
" motor cover	"	Nil			
Eye-plates, for life lines	"	4			
" for rig fittings	"	4			
" of sorts	"	104			
Eyes, lashing	"	13			
Fairleads, metal, transporting	"	4			
" roller	"				
Frames, guard, metal	"				
Fenders (all round, coir rope)	"	Nil			
Fittings to take fire extinguishers	"	14			
Flats, wood, portable	"	60			
Funnel stays (F.S.W.R.) with thimbles shackles, &c.	"	Nil			
G.O.	"	3			
Gibbet for steaming, and combined light	"	Nil			
" klaxon horn	"	Nil			
Gongs	"	Nil			
Gratings, wood, light	"	3			
" steel wire	"	Nil			
Gun mounting ring (channel section)	"				
Gunthwart, with steel girders, stays and bottle screws, &c., complete	"	Nil			

‡ Here insert the Description, Length, and Number of Boat in which the articles are fitted

S.—1401.} (Outside). O.—2.}

Naval Armament and Torpedo Store Accounts
VOUCHER FORM—*Outside Sheet*

† Invoice No. .... † Date of Reporting .... † Return Note No. .... Date ....

Issue Voucher — Section † No. Date — Mode of Conveyance *Hand* — Actual date of Issue *18.8.44* — Receipt Voucher — Section † No. Date

Issued by .... *MTB HEA* .... at .... *HM Hornet* ....

to .... *HMS Hornet* .... at .... *Gosport* .... the following articles

under Authority .... *DNO* .... dated .... I.O. No. .... date ....
† For use at Depôts only

Ledger Number and Folio	Description of Stores	Stamp, or Pattern Number	Total Quantity	†For use at Depôts only		
				S.	R.	U.
	Helmets Steel					
	Gun box Pattern		*4*			
	RDC MK					

Issued .... 194..
Received .... 194..
Sheets ....
(Signature and Rank.) .... (Date.) ....
Wt 18191/D7790 150m Pads 7/43 H.P. 51-6065

ABOVE **A receipt for additional stores issued to MTB 484 at HMS *Hornet* in Gosport.** *(BMPT Collection, via PNBPT)*

supplies on board, British Power Boat staff would present commissioning gifts to the crew – small handmade gifts, hampers of food or even cigars.

Building a crew

Even once it was commissioned, an MGB was not yet ready for front-line service. The first destination after commissioning was a naval base to further equip the boat with naval stores and armament if this had not already been fitted. Vast quantities of sailing and fighting gear was brought aboard, all of it signed for by the boat's new officers. By the time she was fully equipped, the principal armament was fitted along with RDF equipment. Forward of the bridge sat the 2-pounder QF Mk IIC on a Mk XV power-operated mounting. The twin 20mm Oerlikons were fitted in a Mk V power-operated mounting fixed to the wheelhouse, and finally, at the stern, sat the Holman Projector. Small racks on the gunwale were supplied for depth charges amidships and mounts for twin Lewis guns were installed on the deck on either side of the bridge.

The next destination was a 'working-up' base. Working up a boat was necessary to give the crew a chance to train, to practise working together and to put the ship through its paces. It might be done by a group of vessels joining the same flotilla if their commissions had been relatively close together, although often vessels from different flotillas and boat yards undertook the work singly.

In the first years of the war, little thought had been given to training crews or flotillas. In fact, there was not much training that could be provided as there was no weight of experience or policy to fall back on to guide new crews. Basic crew training was given at Fort William in Scotland and some flotillas were formed by gathering boats at one port (usually Fowey in Cornwall) for exercises, but these did not go far enough. At operational bases, crews and commanders who had largely been forced to make up tactics or experiment with their techniques were now having great success and, by 1942, it was evident that Coastal Forces' role in maritime warfare had become both specialised and unique. What was needed was a dedicated facility to train MTB and MGB crews in the peculiarities of their new vessels.

In September 1942, HMS *Bee*, a shore establishment at Weymouth, was commissioned as Coastal Forces' principal working-up base under the tutelage of Commander R.F.B. Swinley, a veteran of the First World War who had subsequently commanded destroyers and aircraft carriers. Several officers with experience of Coastal Forces operations formed the teaching staff, usually on short-term rotations during rests from long periods on operations. The base occupied Weymouth Pavilion at the end of the harbour's pier, along with a hotel and a number of properties alongside the old harbour. Boats were usually moored in the old harbour along Custom House Quay. In October 1943, as preparations for Operation Overlord got under way, HMS *Bee* was relocated to Holyhead in Wales.

Coastal Forces vessels would typically spend up to five weeks working up, although this could take longer in the shorter days of winter. It was a tough business, designed to prepare the crews for the strenuous nature of operational work. Each day the

LEFT **Customs House Quay in June 1944. Landing craft bound for Normandy are moored along the quayside previously used by HMS *Bee*'s MTBs and MGBs.** *(Photos Normandie)*

men would spend time in lectures learning signalling practice, the operation of the boat's equipment, tactics and navigation, followed by practical experience at sea. Gun crews gained experience loading and laying their guns on target while travelling at high speed across lumpy waters and target practice was carried out against moored targets. The radar operator and navigating officer practised plotting an enemy target and directing the skipper and coxswain to intercept it. Engine crews learned to communicate through rudimentary sign language in the noisy confines of the engine room. In groups, the boats would practise formation sailing and group attacks on enemy vessels. During his own working-up at Holyhead, Commander Law recalled that 'The radar operator dreamed of blips and scans all night and the wireless telegraphists fell into their bunks haunted by the sounds of long breaks and obliques.'[3]

Finally, after weeks of training, the base commander would inform the skippers of the boats that he was satisfied they were fully worked up and ready for operations. The boats' next destination would be their operational base.

3   Law, 1989, p. 35.

BELOW **Customs House Quay in 2016. The harbour is little changed since the 1940s, although the boats themselves have. HMS *Blazer* is one of the Royal Navy's P2000 class patrol vessels, the spiritual successors to Coastal Forces.** *(Richard Symonds/ WikiCommons)*

Chapter Three

Anatomy of MGB 81

───●────────────────

Even though she has undergone significant restoration in her life, MGB 81 differs little from her appearance when she was launched in 1942. Although modern technology sits alongside old, the layout of the vessel is not much changed above or below decks. Restored boats such as these offer a glimpse into the cramped conditions under which Coastal Forces crews operated in the 1940s.

OPPOSITE The forward mess, most likely on a 70ft British Power Boat. Note the folding cots above the settees. *(CFHT Collection)*

The hull

Hull design is crucial on a planing boat. Unlike a traditional displacement hull, which pushes water aside as it moves (creating a bow wave), the angled planes of a speedboat force water down as it moves horizontally, which results in a reactionary upwards force on the hull. As speed increases, this lifts the boat out of the water, reducing resistance and allowing for higher speeds over the surface. To achieve this a V-shape hull with a chine will, when driven at speed, create sufficient 'push' down to lift it out of the water. Once clear, the boat essentially surfs on its own bow wave.

The problem with planing hulls is that they tend to be unstable and have insufficient buoyancy to operate at low speeds. The solution sits part-way between a displacement hull and a planing hull – the semi-planing (or semi displacement) hull. The main weight of the boat is supported by buoyancy, but the hull design helps generates lift. Typically, there is a deep narrow V-design to the bow where the chine pushes against the bow wave, but towards the stern the V becomes progressively shallower, culminating in a near-flat bottom at the transom. The line drawings on page 52 demonstrate this progressive change along the length of the Mk V hull. This design of hull is known as hard chine. Towards the stern there is a sharp change in angle between the panels that make up the sides and bottom of the hull. The two lower 'corners' (or chines) are hard angles rather than soft corners more common to a rounded hull.

When driven at speed the bow will lift as the reactive force pushes it up, and the boat will ride on to its bow wave. The flatter stern has more surface area for lifting, which also helps elevate the boat and separates the transom from the stern wave. When the boat is running higher in the water than displacement alone would allow, it is described as riding on the plane.

Planing reduces drag and allows for higher speed with less energy – essentially the boat can travel faster while using less fuel than a displacement hull. On the other hand, planing and semi-planing hulls are inherently less stable than displacement hulls in rough seas. The semi-planing hull will struggle to stay on the plane and as it is driven up by one wave, it tends to crash into the next or the trough between them. In higher sea states, planing becomes impossible and the speed advantages of the semi-planing hull become irrelevant.

The deck

Boarding an MGB from the quayside, you step on to the deck and one thing immediately becomes apparent – the curve. The hog sheer of the deck is visible, but far more noticeable is the lie of the boat. The weight is at the stern with the engines, and therefore here the draught is deeper. Walking forwards from the stern you are literally walking *up* to the bow.

At the bow is the Samson post, the main fixing point for mooring tackle or the boat's anchor. Adjacent to this, the forward access hatch leads into the head compartment below. In 1942 the forward deck area was also used to store the boat's Admiralty CQR-pattern anchor and a life raft, which sat in front of the large, curved breakwater. Today there is a modern anchor assembly on the bow and a life raft remains in front of the breakwater. This raft could be used in an emergency, although it isn't the only safety apparatus on board.

The breakwater shields the deck behind it from spray water cascading over the bow in rough weather. During the war it was crucial to protecting the large 2-pounder pom-pom gun in its power-operated turret. On either side of the gun position were two ready-use lockers – ammunition cases containing ammunition already fitted into magazines to be fed into the gun. Between these and behind the gun a hatch led into the main magazine where further ammunition was kept. Today the replica gun no longer needs ammunition and the ready-use lockers instead hold emergency inflatable life rafts. The access hatch is still in place, but the magazine is no longer in use below, so the hatch is rarely used – except to allow air to ventilate the lower deck when the boat is in harbour.

The gun sits ahead of the wheelhouse,

LEFT MGB 75 at HMS *Beehive* in December 1943. *(IWM A13631)*

along the sides of which are vents to the engine room below. Two ready-use ammunition lockers sit below the 20mm Oerlikon turret – today they disguise further engine room vents. In 1942, on both the port and starboard outer edges of the deck next to the gunwale, sat Mk VII depth charges; meanwhile, towards the stern was a Holman Projector and chemical smoke apparatus. These are no longer fitted, but the lifeline is still in place at the stern. Two simple stanchions support a cable above the transom: it is too low to function as a railing – rather it provides a grab point in case anyone should slip off the stern in rough weather.

BELOW MGB 81 on her post-refit trials in October 2018. *(PNBPT)*

RIGHT The general
arrangement of a 1942
Mk V MGB, drawn from
the original plans by
Al Ross. *(Al Ross)*

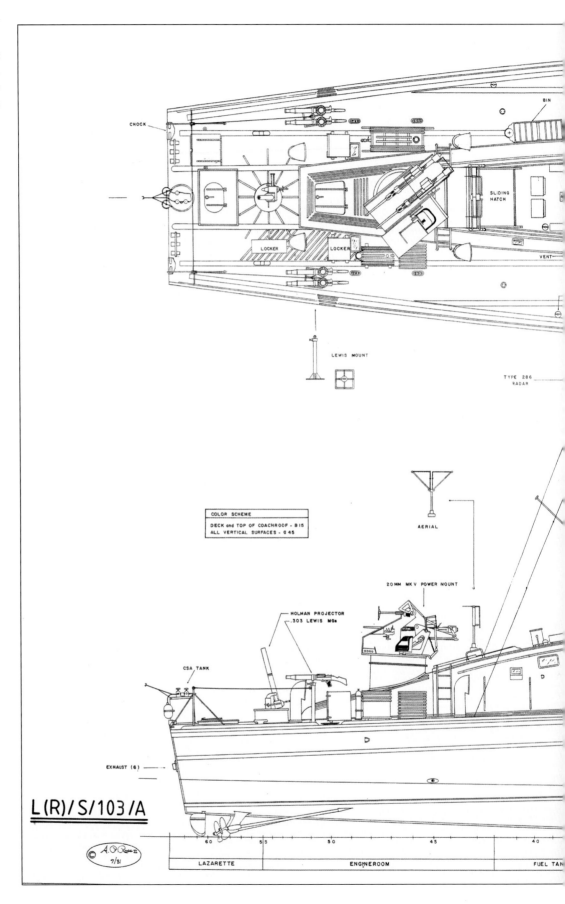

CHOCK

BIN

SLIDING
HATCH

LOCKER   LOCKER

VENT

LEWIS MOUNT

TYPE 286
RADAR

COLOR SCHEME

DECK and TOP OF COACHROOF - B15
ALL VERTICAL SURFACES - G45

AERIAL

20 MM MK V POWER MOUNT

HOLMAN PROJECTOR
.303 LEWIS MGs

CSA TANK

EXHAUST (6)

L(R)/S/103/A

60   55   50   45   40

A.O.Ross II
7/81

LAZARETTE   ENGINEROOM   FUEL TAN

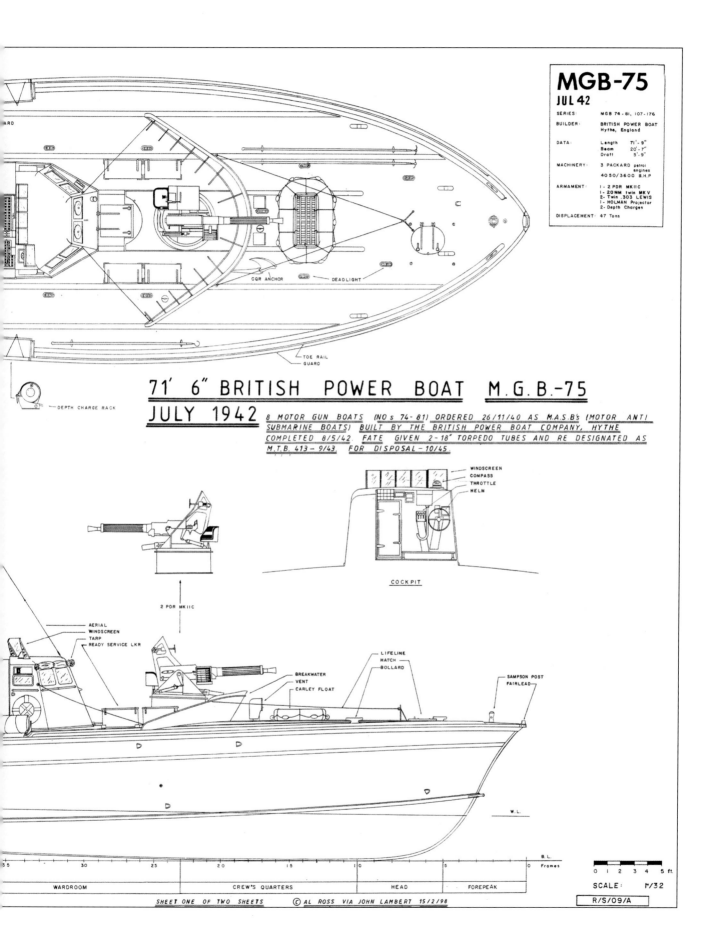

MGB-75
JUL 42

SERIES:	MGB 74-81, 107-176
BUILDER:	BRITISH POWER BOAT Hythe, England
DATA:	Length 71'-9" Beam 20'-7" Draft 5'-9"
MACHINERY:	3 PACKARD petrol engines 4050/3600 B.H.P
ARMAMENT:	1 - 2 PDR MKIIC 1 - 20MM twin MK V 2 - Twin .303 LEWIS 1 - HOLMAN Projector 2 - Depth Charges
DISPLACEMENT:	47 Tons

CQR ANCHOR

DEADLIGHT

TOE RAIL
GUARD

DEPTH CHARGE RACK

71' 6" BRITISH POWER BOAT M.G.B.-75
JULY 1942

8 MOTOR GUN BOATS (NOs 74-81) ORDERED 26/11/40 AS M.A.S.B's (MOTOR ANTI SUBMARINE BOATS) BUILT BY THE BRITISH POWER BOAT COMPANY, HYTHE COMPLETED 8/5/42. FATE GIVEN 2-18" TORPEDO TUBES AND RE DESIGNATED AS M.T.B. 413 - 9/43. FOR DISPOSAL - 10/45.

WINDSCREEN
COMPASS
THROTTLE
HELM

2 PDR MKIIC

COCKPIT

AERIAL
WINDSCREEN
TARP
READY SERVICE LKR

LIFELINE
HATCH
BOLLARD

BREAKWATER
VENT
CARLEY FLOAT

SAMPSON POST
FAIRLEAD

W.L.

B.L.

WARDROOM	CREW'S QUARTERS	HEAD	FOREPEAK	

35   30   25   20   15   10   5   0   Frames

0 1 2 3 4 5 ft.

SCALE: 1"/32

R/S/09/A

SHEET ONE OF TWO SHEETS   © AL ROSS VIA JOHN LAMBERT 15/2/98

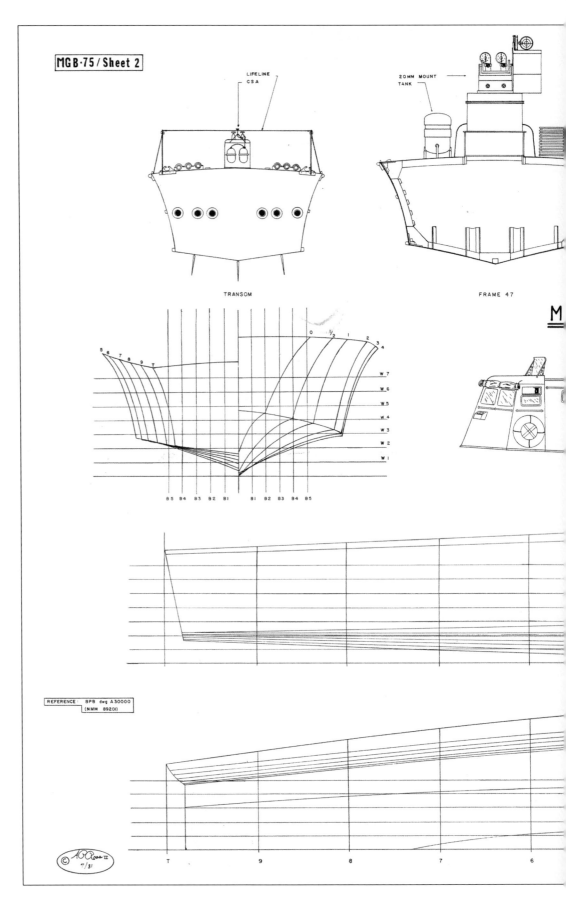

MGB·75 / Sheet 2

LIFELINE
CSA

20MM MOUNT
TANK

TRANSOM

FRAME 47

REFERENCE: BPB dwg A30000
(NMM 89201)

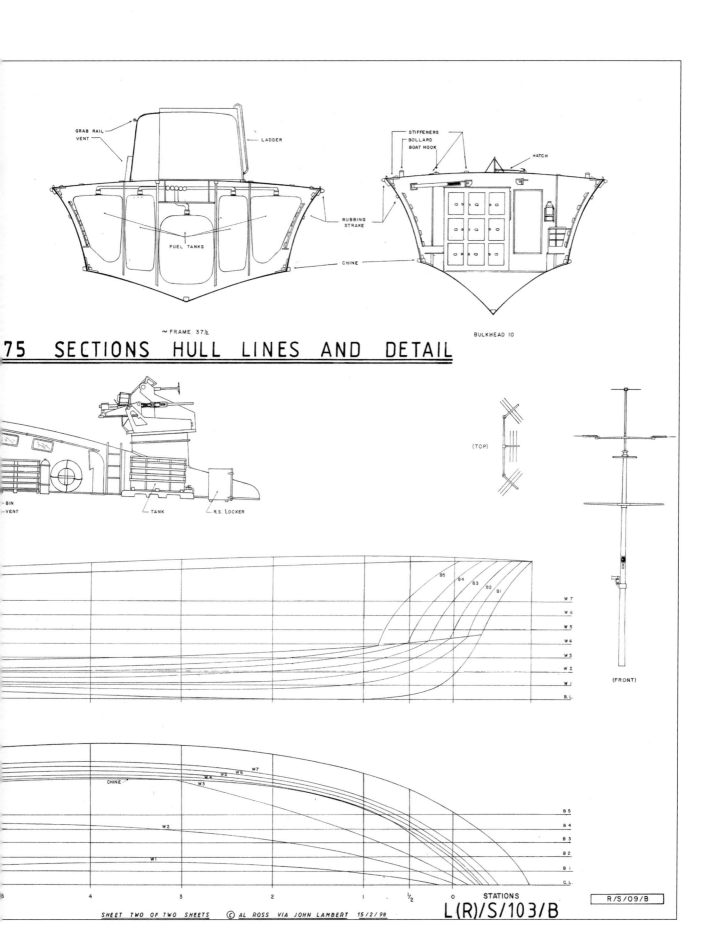

GRAB RAIL
VENT
LADDER
FUEL TANKS
RUBBING STRAKE
CHINE

~ FRAME 37½

STIFFENERS
BOLLARD
BOAT HOOK
HATCH
BULKHEAD 10

75 SECTIONS HULL LINES AND DETAIL

BIN
VENT
TANK
R.S. LOCKER

(TOP)

(FRONT)

CHINE

W7 W6 W5 W4 W3 W2 W1 B.L.

B5 B4 B3 B2 B1

W7 W6 W5 W4 W3 W2 W1

B5 B4 B3 B2 B1 C.L.

STATIONS

R/S/09/B

SHEET TWO OF TWO SHEETS   © AL ROSS VIA JOHN LAMBERT   15/2/98   L(R)/S/103/B

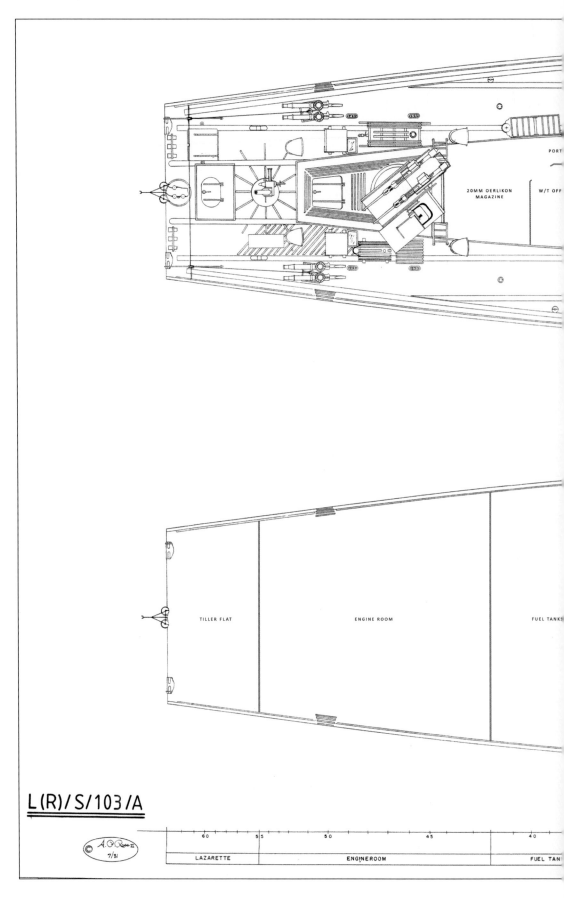

RIGHT Plan of Mk V MGB wheelhouse and below deck, modified from the original general arrangement by Al Ross. *(Al Ross)*

20MM OERLIKON MAGAZINE

PORT

W/T OFF

L(R)/S/103/A

TILLER FLAT

ENGINE ROOM

FUEL TANKS

LAZARETTE

ENGINEROOM

FUEL TAN

60   55   50   45   40

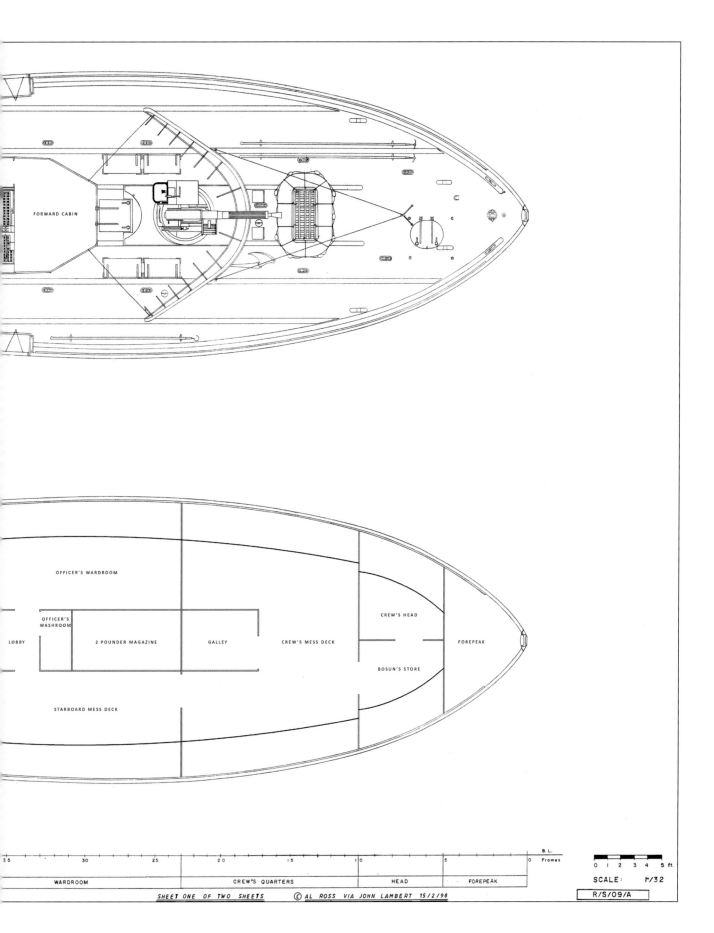

FORWARD CABIN

OFFICER'S WARDROOM

OFFICER'S WASHROOM

CREW'S HEAD

LOBBY

2 POUNDER MAGAZINE

GALLEY

CREW'S MESS DECK

FOREPEAK

BOSUN'S STORE

STARBOARD MESS DECK

B. L.

35   30   25   20   15   10   5   0   Frames

WARDROOM   CREW'S QUARTERS   HEAD   FOREPEAK

SHEET ONE OF TWO SHEETS   © AL ROSS VIA JOHN LAMBERT 15/2/98

0 1 2 3 4 5 ft.

SCALE: 1"/32

R/S/09/A

No. 1149 FEB. 26th, 1983.
Every Monday.

Victor

14p
I.R. 21p
(Inc. VAT)

A TRUE STORY OF MEN 'AT' WAR

They called them the Mile-a-Minute Mariners, those seamen of the Royal Navy's small craft during the Second World War. They patrolled the North Sea and the English Channel in all weathers, protecting coastal convoys, attacking enemy shipping, and fighting it out with their opposite numbers of Germany's E-boat command.

In the summer of 1942, the 8th Flotilla Motor Gun Boats, under Lieutenant Commander R.P. Hitchens, set off on a routine patrol towards the Channel Islands...

HALF AHEAD, COURSE 190. ALL BOATS LINE ASTERN!

The patrol was nearly ended and dawn was in the eastern sky when...

NAVIGATION LIGHTS OFF THE PORT BOW, SIR!

ACHTUNG, BRITISH GUNBOATS, OPEN FIRE IMMEDIATELY!

IT'S TWO JERRY ARMED TRAWLERS.

CONTINUED ON BACK PAGE

As Mk V Motor Gun Boat

Dimensions

Length:	71ft 6in (official classification, although in fact the peak of the gunwale extended the overall length of the Mk V by 3in to 71ft 9in)
Beam:	20ft 7in
Draught:	2ft 11in forward, 5ft 9in aft
Displacement:	37 tons unladen, 46.6 tons laden

Machinery

3 × Packard 4M-2500 marine petrol engines, each of 1,250hp, 1:1 direct drive (centre engine), vee drive (wing engines)	
1 × Ford 10hp auxiliary engine	
Fuel:	2,733 gallons of 100-octane petrol
Range:	475nm at 35kts, 550nm at 20kts, 600nm at 15kts
Speed (on trials):	Maximum emergency speed (2,400rpm): 38.63kts
	Maximum continuous speed (2,000rpm): 34.75kts

Armament

1942 (as built)
1 × Mk IIC 40mm 2-pounder pom-pom (Mk XV power-operated mounting)
1 × twin 20mm Oerlikon (Mk V power-operated mounting)
2 × twin 0.303 in Lewis machine guns
2 × Mk VII depth charges
1 × Holman Projector
1944 (at Normandy)
1 × Mk VIII 40mm Vickers (Mk XVI power-operated mounting)
1 × twin Oerlikon (Mk IX hand-operated mounting)
2 × twin 0.303in Vickers machine guns
50 × Mk XIII depth charges

Crew

2 or 3 officers, 10 to 12 crew
Commanding Officer (usually a lieutenant or sub-lieutenant)
First Lieutenant (usually a sub-lieutenant)
Coxswain (the senior enlisted crewman, usually a petty officer or leading seaman)
Leading stoker (engine room)
Stoker (engine room)
Telegraphist/Signaller (W/T and RDF office)
Able seamen (two or more – primarily gun crew)
Ordinary seamen (four or more – primarily gun crew)

Timeline

Ordered as 70ft MA/SB:	27 November 1940
Order modified to 71ft 6in Mk V MGB:	February 1941
Laid down:	16 December 1941
Launched:	26 June 1942
Trials:	8 July 1942
Commissioned:	11 July 1942
Approved to lay up:	5 March 1945
Paid off:	27 April 1945
Taken in hand for de-equipping:	10 May 1945
Approval to dispose:	2 October 1945
Handed over to Director of Small Craft Disposals:	25 October 1945

2020 Specification

Machinery

3 × Italian FPT Cursor 13 Mermaid marine diesel engines, each of 825hp, 1:1 direct drive (centre engine), vee drive (wing engines)	
1 × Cummins Onan QD 7/9kW marine generator, with three-cylinder, four-stroke, water-cooled Kubota diesel engine	
Speed:	Maximum continuous speed (2,500rpm): 34kts

The bridge

The bridge is the nerve centre for any vessel and the Mk V MGB was no exception. The bridge sits at the forward end of the wheelhouse, above and behind the forward cabin and slightly offset to starboard – this provides space for the access passage down the port side of the wheelhouse. The bridge is open – there is no roof and it could be a wet place in rough weather – so duck boards are fitted to the floor. An angled windscreen reduces the airflow and spray to the front.

Today the bridge of MGB 81 is little different to how it originally appeared in 1942. Perhaps the most significant change is the access: originally, there was no starboard side door on to the deck. Instead access to the deck was via a short ladder across the starboard side armour plating, making the bridge entirely enclosed. This design of bridge contrasts with the open MTB-type bridge of Vosper and Fairmile boats and led to the 'dustbin bridge' name among crews. Today, with less chance of receiving fire from S-boats, a simple door makes access easier.

ABOVE The bridge of MGB 81 in her present (2020) configuration. Almost all controls are centralised on the bridge. *(PNBPT)*

BELOW The bridge layout on a 70ft British Power Boat, MGB 16. The helm is on the left-hand side – the small steering wheel is just out of sight below the telegraphs. The instrument panel is simple as most of the engine displays are in the engine room. A door to starboard provides access into the small wheelhouse. *(Peter Scott)*

LEFT **This image shows how things have changed on the Mk V boat (in this case on MTB 450). The offset to starboard, allowing room for the port-side passageway, is clearly visible. Curiously, although the vessel drawings show the Admiralty Pattern Compass 1151 A on the starboard side of the bridge in front of the helm, here it has been moved to the port forward corner side of the bridge, which makes it difficult for the helmsman to use. This could well have been a modification requested by the commanding officer when standing by the boat at British Power Boat, although it might simply be that the compass case cover has been removed from the mount on the starboard side!** *(Christopher Timms)*

BELOW This photograph shows the bridge of MTB 482, a Mk VI boat. The MTB wheelhouse centralises the bridge again as there is no port side passageway.
The helm remains on the starboard side but now all control is on the bridge, with gear levers on the port side of the access door into the forward cabin and throttles on the starboard. A voice pipe sits between the two with two torpedo firing levers alongside – a reminder of the MGB's new role. *(Christopher Timms)*

Also on the starboard side is the helm, exactly where it was when MGB 81 was launched in 1942. Originally the position was equipped with the main wheel, a compass in front of the helmsman, an instrument panel and combined telegraphs and engine throttles. Today it is little changed, although the technology is improved. Separate throttle and gear levers flank the instrument panel, while the compass is joined by a modern digital display. The steering was, and remains, mechanical, the wheel connected to the rudders through a system of bars and linkages that pass through the hull.

The port side of the bridge (in reality the centre of the wheelhouse) provided extra space for crew, a flag locker and the access door down into the forward cabin.

The forward cabin

M any early small boats built by British Power Boat, Vosper, Thornycroft and J. Samuel White placed the vessels' main controls in enclosed wheelhouses. It was from here that the boat was driven – the bridge was a platform for the commanding officer to direct the boat (although duplicate steering was also fitted). Originally, then, this forward cabin was the actual wheelhouse, although that name is more often applied to the entire above-deck structure.

By the early 1940s, operational experience had shown that control was better exercised from the bridge and when Selman designed his new MGBs, duplicate controls were found there. The wheelhouse also had a secondary role – as an enclosed and dry space it functioned as the chart room in which the first lieutenant or third officer could plot the boat's journey and location.

While satellite navigation simplifies the job today, navigating during the Second World War was no easy task. The navigator was constantly being fed the compass bearings the boat was headed on and the engine revolutions, so that he could determine the speed and therefore the distance travelled. Factors such as the wind, sea state and the running tide would add additional complications to these calculations, and as soon as the boat came into contact with the enemy the rapid manoeuvres and course changes could make his job exceedingly difficult. Only when recognisable features such as buoys or lighthouses (when illuminated) were sighted could a firm fix be established.

Nonetheless, well-trained navigators could accurately plot their journeys to within a few hundred metres. In his memoir, *Night Action*, Peter Dickens, CO of the 21st MTB Flotilla (and great-grandson of author Charles Dickens), recalled crossing the North Sea in March 1943 when his group of three boats came across two large barrels of Guinness floating in the water. Knowing that they couldn't take the large barrels with them to the Dutch coast, his navigator Lieutenant Alan Jensen marked the spot on his charts. After a quiet patrol, Jensen led the flotilla back to the barrels and, despite their own movement with the tide and wind – and a fog – they were found and recovered.

In 1942 the MGB's controls were located on the forward port side of the cabin. On the starboard side was a large chart table over three chart drawers. In front of this and against the back wall was the hatch that led down into the accommodation areas forward of the fuel tanks, while the port side passageway led to the wireless transmission (W/T) office.

By the end of the war the wheelhouse no longer functioned as such in any way, with many boatbuilders moving all control to the bridge and leaving the forward cabin solely

ABOVE The chart table on MGB 81 still serves the same function, although it now benefits from more modern technology. *(Author)*

LEFT The access hatch to the forward accommodation areas has been moved slightly forward from its original location. When closed, the duckboard covering prevents accidents. *(Author)*

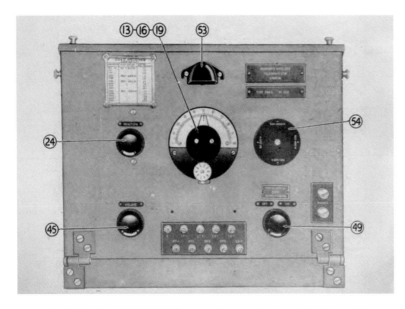

ABOVE The Type TW12A W/T set was the standard model in Coastal Forces vessels in the early years of the war. *(HMS Collingwood Heritage Collection)*

BELOW The Type 291U RDF set, fitted into Coastal Forces vessels in the later years of the war. *(HMS Collingwood Heritage Collection)*

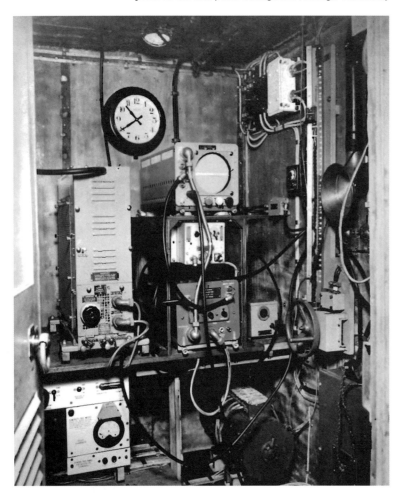

as a chart room. With less need for backup controls on MGB 81 today, the forward cabin functions purely as the chart room. The chart table is arranged slightly differently in the starboard rear corner, but serves much the same function as it did in 1942, now aided by GPS technology. The only other significant change is the location of the hatch, which has been moved slightly forward.

The W/T office

The space in the wheelhouse was incredibly tight, as illustrated by the narrow side passage and the access to the small W/T office cabin behind the bridge. This was the domain of the signaller. In theory signalling between ships was via one of three methods – the W/T set, Morse lamp or signalling flags. In practice Morse lamps were rarely used – a bright light flickering across the sea at night would, of course, compromise the clandestine nature of Coastal Forces operations. Similarly, the flag locker on the bridge was of little use in the dark.

The signaller therefore spent most of his time in the W/T office. In the early years of the war the standard set in Coastal Forces boats was the 1935 Type TW12A and its associated 394E receiver. The set only permitted communication by Morse code rather than spoken word. The equipment and its power supply was large and took up most of the forward port corner of the office. Later it was replaced with radio telephone (R/T) equipment, allowing voice communication between boats and shore stations. It also made it possible to monitor enemy frequencies and often MTBs and MGBs took German speakers with them on patrol to listen to the enemy's conversations. This new form of intelligence acquired the nickname 'Headache' and proved extremely useful when attempting to intercept enemy vessels.

On MGB 81, the signaller had an additional task. The Mk V boats were among the first to be equipped with RDF equipment – an early form of radar. Coastal Forces boats were equipped with Type 286U, a version that was developed from the small ASV (air-to-surface vessel) Mk II sets that were installed in aircraft. This ASV type was first converted for use in

ABOVE An illustration from the 1945 Admiralty Radar Manual (CB 4182/45), showing the aerials of (1) the Type 291U RDF and (2) the Type 242 IFF interrogator. Many wartime photographs had details such as these obscured by censors.
(HMS Collingwood Heritage Collection)

RIGHT Today the W/T office is less cluttered and serves as the main electrical room. *(Author)*

BELOW Items that need to be quickly accessed from the bridge are usually stored in the W/T room. *(Author)*

large warships such as destroyers in 1940, but it took time for them to become available to small boats. Fitting it to Coastal Forces boats also significantly reduced its range: use in an aircraft could be effective from between 15 and 25 miles, while in an MGB this was reduced to just 2 miles.

The RDF aerials were fitted to the mast but were fixed and did not rotate. The RDF only worked in one direction – forwards – with weak transmission/reception signals about 15 degrees off the bow. If the RDF operator picked up a signal, he would need to direct the boat until he had the strongest echo, which would indicate the target was dead ahead.

RDF evolved quickly. The Type 286PU introduced rotatable aerials, turned by a hand crank in the W/T office, and the Type 252 interrogator introduced an identification friend or foe (IFF) system. To differentiate between friendly and enemy targets identified by RDF, low-powered transponders in Allied ships would be activated by friendly RDF waves and emit a signal of their own, creating a pulsating echo on the interrogating set. If there was no response, the target was likely to be an enemy vessel.

The RDF was primitive and temperamental, but after being guided to a target from a shore station, it made it possible to identify other vessels in the darkness of the night. Later, most British Power Boat vessels had their sets replaced by Type 291U, an updated version with an improved receiver. At the same time, the increasing size of the equipment made the small cabin almost impossible to work in and there was considerable interference between the W/T and the RDF. By way of remedy, when the Mk VI boat came into service it had separate W/T and RDF cabins.

Today, the modern (and significantly smaller) GPS, sonar and radio equipment occupies the forward cabin. The W/T office is instead used for the boat's main electrics and as a store.

Aft wheelhouse space

The aftmost space in the wheelhouse is too small and cramped for anything other than storage and the forward access hatch to the engine room. In 1942 this space was the magazine for the 20mm Oerlikon turret further aft.

Accommodation areas

Access to the forward accommodation areas is through the hatch in the forward cabin. The ladder descends into a small lobby area providing access to the small officers' wardroom on the port side of the boat, and crew's mess on the starboard.

Wardroom

On any Royal Navy vessel it is normal for the officers and ratings to have separate accommodation areas and, despite their diminutive size, MGBs were no exception. That said, the wardroom on MGB 81 was necessarily sparse and consisted of little more than two settee berths, two small wardrobes and a folding table. The settee berths had

BELOW The wardroom looking aft towards the bulkhead at frame 36. The two berths are in their settee arrangement with locker stowage underneath. At the rear bulkhead, behind which are the fuel tanks, the steering mechanism can be seen running from the bridge to the hull. From here it passes through the fuel tank space and engine room to the stern of the boat. *(Author)*

lockers for storage underneath and could be converted into beds, although this was by and large unnecessary in home waters as accommodation was usually provided ashore.

Starboard side mess

Heading to the starboard side of the vessel from the lobby leads into the crew mess area. The aft space was sometimes allocated to the coxswain and leading ratings. Again, the space was basic, with storage under the settee berths. Unlike the officers' space, folding cots were positioned above the settees. These could be raised to provide seating space on the settees or lowered to provide two more sleeping berths for the crew.

The berths are actually positioned on a vital part of the ship's hull. The front of the settee is on one of the longitudinal girders that runs the length of the vessel and is duplicated in the port side officers' wardroom.

Crew's mess

Forward of the starboard space there is access to the main crew mess. In 1942 a watertight door would have provided access through the bulkhead, although that is no longer necessary today.

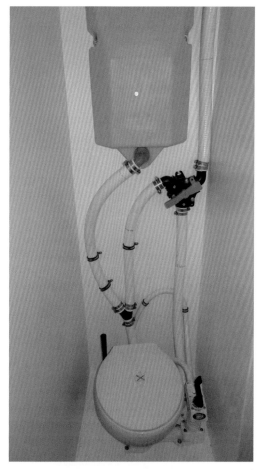

LEFT The toilets on MGB 81 are much more modern than those installed in 1942. *(Author)*

LEFT Looking aft in the starboard side mess deck towards the bulkhead at frame 36. *(Author)*

RIGHT **Looking aft into the crew mess deck. In 1942 folding cots sat above the settee berths, although they were rarely used. In the centre of the space the two longitudinal bulkheads frame the small galley. The bulkhead running between the crew space and the officers' wardroom (starboard side) sits at frame 23.** *(Author)*

The mess was fitted with another four settee berths above which were folding cots, providing a total of eight more sleeping spaces for the crew. In total the MGB could accommodate 14 men, although this was seldom necessary. At bases around the UK, boat crew were almost always accommodated ashore in requisitioned buildings, dormitories or hotels, or on board parent vessels that acted as an HQ in some of the more remote bases (the requisitioned steam merchant ship HMS *Aberdonian* provided officer accommodation at Dartmouth for example). The mess instead functioned as the crew's social space, where meals could be served from the galley on to the central folding table. Against the forward bulkhead were nine lockers, usually enough for the number of crew in this area of the boat.

The galley

The mess is partially split by the central compartment projecting from the aft bulkhead.

LEFT **Looking from the galley into the magazine space. Originally these two compartments were separated by the bulkhead at frame 23, but this has been penetrated on the modern layout to provide extra access to the lobby area.** *(Author)*

This is formed by the two longitudinal bulkheads that Selman included to support the weight of the 2-pounder pom-pom gun on the deck. Between them, the two bulkheads enclose additional compartments in the centre of the accommodation area. At the forward end is the galley.

The boat's galley was a simple affair consisting of a small work surface, a sink, a tea urn and a small stove. In some Coastal Forces boats the stove was a primus fuel stove fitted to a gimbal to keep it steady, but by 1942 electric hotplates, which were far less dangerous, were in use.

Although accommodation was less necessary on these boats, hot food and drink was still essential on long night-time patrols. There was no dedicated cook among the crew of the boat – instead men would usually be allocated galley duty on a rotation or, if a competent crewman demonstrated his prowess, he might become the permanent unofficial chef.

The magazine

Astern of the galley and separated by a bulkhead, the central compartment between the longitudinal bulkheads functioned as the main magazine for the 2-pounder pom-

pom gun. A hatch above provided access to the rear of the gun, making it easy to pass ammunition up to restock the ready-use lockers.

Today, free of the need to keep ammunition aboard, the galley has been extended through the bulkhead to provide an extra work and storage space, as well as easier access to the main hatch.

MGB armament

As a gun boat, MGB 81's armament was skewed towards heavy firepower. In 1940 the heaviest armaments to be found on Coastal Forces boats were 0.303in Vickers machine guns. Progressively 0.5in Vickers machine guns became available, along with small numbers of 20mm Oerlikons. Some pre-war weaponry also began to be installed on Fairmile Bs, including QF 3-pounder Hotchkiss guns and 2-pounder Rolls-Royce guns. Throughout the war, commanders tried different weapons as they became available – Lieutenant Commander Robert Hichens, commander of the 6th and 8th MGB Flotillas, even used a Blacker Bombard, an anti-tank spigot mortar, on more than one occasion – including on the night he was killed.

In 1941 heavier armament began to be

ABOVE Officers of the 29th (Canadian) MTB Flotilla inspect a Vickers Mk VIII 2-pounder pom-pom on a Mk XVI power mounting. *(Library and Archives Canada/ PA-143046)*

installed on Fairmile C MGBs, including 2-pounder pom-pom guns. At the same time more Oerlikons were being manufactured and both these weapons would form the basis of the Mk V's armament. Technically they had both been introduced as anti-aircraft guns, but they were of sufficient calibre, range and rate of fire to perform admirably in small-ship surface actions.

2-pounder pom-pom gun

The QF (Quick Firing) 2-pounder gun can trace its roots back to the Boer War when the QF 1-pounder, designed by Sir Hiram Maxim in the late 1880s, was used by the Boers against the British. Impressed by the performance of the weapon, the British had the design copied by Vickers and in 1915

they produced a larger version for the Royal Navy – the 2-pounder. Officially an autocannon (or small artillery piece) the gun fired small 2lb high-explosive rounds of 40mm calibre with an effective range of 1,000m. Supplied by 25-round fabric ammunition belts, it fired at a rate of 200 rounds/min, which could be sustained for some time with its water-cooled barrel. This did make it a heavy weapon, though – with its hand mounting it weighed more than 700kg. Although a successful anti-aircraft weapon, it had its drawbacks, which the Mk II*C attempted to rectify by introducing 14-round metal belts that could be linked together to increase the ammunition feed. Its steady rhythmic rate of fire quickly earned it the nickname 'pom-pom', by which it and following marks became universally known.

Numerous Mk II*Cs were still in service in the Second World War and Marine Mountings Ltd created a Mk XV power mounting in order to equip Coastal Forces vessels. Only 28 of these were ever made, but the first flotilla of Mk V boats, including MGB 81, were fitted with them in 1942.

The Mk II*C was soon replaced as an improved model became available. Design work on an updated 2-pounder suitable for multiple-barrel mountings had been ongoing since the early 1920s and finally, a decade later, the improved gun began to be fitted on ships as an anti-aircraft defence in mountings of up to eight guns. The Mk VIII was a considerable improvement over the Mk II*C and increased the effective range of the weapon to over 1,500m. Multi-barrel mountings could supply the gun from 140-round magazines and it became a dependable and effective anti-aircraft gun throughout the Second World War.

Marine Mountings once again designed a power-operated single-barrel mount for Coastal Forces, the Mk XVI. Fitted with a 56-round magazine, the gun had a rate of fire of 115 round/min and a muzzle velocity of 732m/sec. Hydraulic power came from the boat's main engines, allowing the gun to train at a speed of 40 degrees per second, or elevate at 25 degrees per second. The hydraulic pipes ran along the deckheads below, but here they were vulnerable to enemy gunfire – later

BELOW A Vickers Mk VIII 2-pounder pom-pom on a Mk XVI power mounting.

models saw the pipes run along the keel, but the risk of losing power to the turret altogether never went away, and was inevitable when the boat was stopped. Although the rear turret was later replaced with a hand-trained mount, the 1,110kg weight of the forward gun meant that this was never an option. Ammunition was usually a combination of high-explosive (HE) and HE tracer, vital for night actions so that the gunlayer could see where his rounds were going. Armour-piercing (AP) ammunition was also used, which was especially useful against the bridges of S-boats.

6-pounder

On later MTBs the 2-pounder was replaced by the 6-pounder Mk IIA Molins gun. A development of the hand-loaded Royal Artillery 6-pounder anti-tank gun, the naval version was fitted with the Molins power-loading six-round autoloader that fired at a rate of one round a second. With a muzzle velocity of 655m/sec and a maximum range of 5,600m, the 57mm HE shell could do considerable damage to a target.

Fitted to a Mk VII mounting (very similar in appearance to the 2-pounder's Mk XVI), the gun weighed 1,747kg, a testament to the reinforcement Selman had made to the hull of his boats.

20mm Oerlikon

The Oerlikon had a troubled start in Royal Navy service. The weapon's origins dated back to a German design from the First World War. In the 1920s the rights to produce the gun were acquired by the Swiss firm Oerlikon,

BELOW A 6-pounder Mk IIA Molins gun on a Mk VII mounting.

who enhanced it into the most up-to-date 20mm gun in the world. The gun was sold globally and in 1937 was presented to the Admiralty. Few officers took much interest, but Lord Louis Mountbatten, then serving in the Naval Air Division of the Admiralty, instantly saw its potential. Overcoming obstruction and red tape, he arranged for a demonstration of the gun by fitting it to MTB 102 in Portsmouth and in 1939 an order for 1,500 guns was placed with Oerlikon.

Ironically, Switzerland obtained the steel for the gun barrels from Germany. Although the German government must have realised that some of the raw material they were supplying to Switzerland during the Phoney War was going to their enemy, they appear to have made little effort to disrupt supply. Nonetheless, it was obvious that in order to secure greater numbers of the gun, it would be necessary to get the technical details and drawings of it to Britain. This was achieved by Steuart Mitchell, a member of staff of the Chief Inspector of Naval Ordnance, who escaped from Switzerland through the Balkans, Turkey, Palestine and Egypt, before flying back to England. Within a year, Britain was producing 750 Oerlikons a month, rising to 1,000 in 1942. It was only then that there were sufficient numbers available to satisfy the competing needs of the RAF and Royal Navy, and they began to be equipped as standard on Coastal Forces vessels.

The Oerlikon had a rate of fire of up to 480 rounds/min and a maximum range of more than 6,000m. It used a mix of HE tracer and HE incendiary, fed by a 60-round drum magazine. Marine Mountings designed the Mk V mounting to fit a pair of guns in a power-operated turret, driven by oil pressure from pumps in the engine room. Like the forward

LEFT A hand-trained twin Oerlikon mount on a Mk VI MTB. The metal frame prevents the gunner from accidentally firing on to the MTB's bridge.
(Library and Archives Canada/PA-144581)

gun, this made them vulnerable to enemy gunfire and the risk of losing power to the turret was a significant problem on early boats.

This was overcome, partly at the insistence of men like Hichens, by the turret's replacement with a hand-trained mounting. In Felixstowe, HMS *Beehive*'s gunnery officer, Lieutenant Woods, created a simple cradle to mount a second barrel on a hand-trained mount. Operational experience quickly revealed that the mount was no harder to operate with two barrels than one. At 570kg, the Mk IX (manual) mounting was nearly 700kg lighter than the power-operated one, and by reducing the weight in the boat elsewhere (particularly the excessive weight of spare ammunition) it was possible to fit torpedo tubes to the Mk Vs.

Lewis guns

The final gun armament on the MGBs were twin machine guns fitted either side of the bridge. Initially these were Lewis guns, a weapon dating back to the First World War. Later these were replaced by Vickers K machine guns, a lightweight gas-operated gun that could fire up to 1,200 rounds/min.

Both guns fired the standard British .303in rifle round, which had little penetrating power compared to the forward 2-pounder and the aft 20mm Oerlikons. However, they were useful additional weapons for sweeping the decks of enemy vessels in close combat, forcing enemy crewmen to take cover. Equally the exposed position of the guns on the MGB's deck, with no form of cover or protection, meant that casualties among the machine gunners were high.

Holman Projector

The Holman Projector, named after its designer Treve Holman of Holman Brothers Ltd, was a simple anti-aircraft weapon that used compressed air to fire a small explosive charge into the air. The early models of this weapon fired hand grenades but the version fitted to Coastal Forces boats, the Mk III, could fire several in one go. In fact it could fire just about anything that could fit down the barrel. It is said that at a demonstration attended by Prime Minister Winston Churchill, when it was discovered that no ammunition had

been supplied, full bottles of beer were used instead, providing suitable frothy explosions on the target.

Coastal Forces crews found the devices to be fairly useless in combat and, it is said, mostly used them to fire potatoes at each other as their boats returned from patrol. Hichens, however, found another use for them – launching flares. He had several discussions with Holman and sketched out an idea for a Mk IV projector with a shorter barrel and a swivel mount. A prototype was mocked up for Hichens to use, but he was killed before he had a chance to test it. The Mk IV never went into production, but Hichens's use of the weapon later led to the introduction of dedicated flare guns on Coastal Forces boats.

Depth charges

Depth charges are usually thought of as anti-submarine weapons and it's true that that's where their genesis in the First World War lay. However, they were also a useful weapon against surface vessels when detonated at a suitable depth: if dropped ahead of a vessel so that it would detonate under the hull when it was sailed across, the explosion could

LEFT **An early model of a Holman Projector.** *(Crown Copyright)*

break the keel and sink the vessel. In practice this was easier said than done – the depth charge was detonated by a hydrostatic pistol activated by water pressure at a certain depth. To do damage to a surface vessel this would need to be set shallow, leaving a narrow window between dropping the charge and it detonating. To achieve success, the attacker would need to release the charge close to the bow of the enemy ship.

Most Coastal Forces boats, including MGBs and MTBs, were equipped with a pair, or sometimes more, of Mk VII depth charges. These were carried in cradles on the gunwale of the boat and usually held in place with straps, but once these were removed the charge could be pushed over the side using a simple lever mechanism on the bridge. Despite its small size, the Mk VII carried a powerful kick – it contained 130kg of Amatol explosive and weighed 191kg overall. It sank at a speed of 2m/sec and could be set to explode at various depths in 15m increments. Operational use proved that its sinking speed was too slow when attacking U-boats and extra weights were fitted to speed the descent; however, the problem was quite the opposite for MGBs attacking ships – the charge sank too quickly. This necessitated dropping the charge right under the bow of an enemy ship – a risky manoeuvre – in order to successfully detonate it beneath the keel. When a charge was dropped to sink or discourage a pursuing vessel, it wasn't unheard of that empty oil drums would be attached to it in order to slow the descent sufficiently that it would detonate near the surface.

In 1944 several MTBs were equipped with timber racks carrying up to 48 Mk XII depth charges. These were fitted with a 25kg charge of Minol and were intended only for use against midget submarines, which operated extensively in the Bay of Seine during the summer of 1944.

Torpedoes

Mk V boats that had been lightened by the removal of the rear power-operated turret, as well as the revamped Mk VI boats, could be equipped with a pair of 18in Mk II torpedo tubes, one on each side of the bridge.

The torpedo tube so recognisable on MTBs evolved from a simple design produced by Thornycroft that was improved upon by the Royal Navy's torpedo school at HMS *Vernon*. The Mk I tube was soon followed by the Mk II, of which some 2,000 were produced for 18in and 21in torpedoes during the war. The torpedo was loaded through the rear of the tube and fired by a small explosive charge in the attachment at the rear. The charge was fired using levers on the bridge, but should there be a malfunction, ratings were positioned at the back of each tube with a mallet to strike the firing pin.

A variety of torpedoes were carried by MTBs, but the most common was the Mk XV, an 817kg torpedo with a 247kg Torpex charge. It had a range of 2,200m–3,300m and speeds of 30kts–40kts.

Torpedoes were expensive pieces of equipment and not used lightly. A report had to be written out every time one was fired, justifying the use and whether it was successful. In fact Coastal Forces fired 1,169 torpedoes during the war, with 301 probable hits. This was an average success rate of 25.8%, far more successful than submarines (22%) and destroyers (15.6%), and was only surpassed by Fleet Air Arm aircraft (36.4%).

BELOW **A 21in torpedo is lowered on to the deck of MTB 232 at Felixstowe. MTB 232 was part of the 21st MTB Flotilla commanded by Lieutenant Peter Dickens.**

RIGHT AND FAR RIGHT A brand new twin Oerlikon turret, constructed of lightweight aluminium, was manufactured by Hythe Marine Services in 2015. *(Tiger Juden)*

ABOVE LEFT Fortunately, MGB 81's restoration between 1998 and 2002 (see Chapter 7) was based on original British Power Boat drawings, and there was a separate panel in the wheelhouse at the location the turret was fitted. *(Tiger Juden)*

ABOVE Extra reinforcement beams were fitted in the engine room to support the weight of the turret. *(Tiger Juden)*

LEFT The turret mount installed into the wheelhouse, ready to receive the twin Oerlikons. As a cosmetic replica, the turret was not designed to rotate. *(Tiger Juden)*

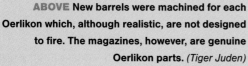

ABOVE New barrels were machined for each Oerlikon which, although realistic, are not designed to fire. The magazines, however, are genuine Oerlikon parts. *(Tiger Juden)*

ABOVE RIGHT The completed twin Oerlikon turret installed. *(Author)*

RIGHT Mounts for the replica depth charges were manufactured in Boathouse 4, in accordance with original drawings. *(Tiger Juden)*

BELOW Marine plywood was used for the construction. Unlike regular ply, marine ply is cross-laminated and more resistant to moisture, owing to its denser construction. The completed mount was finished with epoxy resin for extra durability before it was painted. *(Tiger Juden)*

RIGHT Unlike the original mounts, these would not need to support a 191kg depth charge. Instead, a replica was fitted once the mount was installed on the deck. *(Tiger Juden)*

Head flat

The forwardmost compartment of the boat was known as the head flat or just the heads. On the port side was the crew's ablutions room, which included a toilet and wash facilities, as well as the useful features of a wet room with drip trays for wet oilskins and boots. The starboard side provided storage space, known as the bosun's store, where ropes, repair material, paint and other sundries would be kept. A hatch above provided access to the upper deck, although this was only opened in port and would only be used in an emergency at sea. A small panel provided

access through the foremost bulkhead and into the tiny forepeak space. Abutting the forepart of the keel, this space was usually used as a chain store for the boat's Admiralty CQR-pattern anchor.

Engine room

There were two points of access to the engine room – the forward hatch leading into the aft wheelhouse space, and the aft hatch behind the 20mm Oerlikon turret. MGB 81 was originally equipped with three Packard 4M-2500 marine petrol engines and a Ford auxiliary engine which

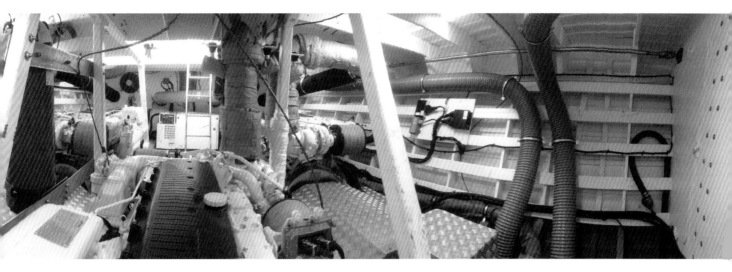

provided power for the boat's electrics. The three Packard main engines were arranged with the centre one positioned forward, connected directly to the central shaft, with the wing engines further aft and facing the other way. The power to their shafts was through short Cardan shafts into vee drives that drove the main shafts running back under the engines. The Ford auxiliary engine sat on the starboard side in the forward space alongside the centre Packard. Opposite, on the port side, was a store of fire extinguishers and all around were seawater cooling-system pipes, exhaust tubes and the fuel lines feeding from the fuel tanks forward.

Today, the equipment is more modern, but the space is very much as it was in 1942. The three Italian FPT Cursor 13 diesel engines sit in the same positions as the original Packards and the gearboxes and vee drives work in the same manner. A few pieces of equipment have been moved around – the generator engine has been repositioned to the rear bulkhead behind the aft hatch ladder, and a modern, much larger automatic fire extinguisher system has been fitted on the forward starboard side. The machinery makes the space incredibly tight, as it was during the war, and movement around the area is difficult. With all three engines running it's also extremely hot and noisy.

Tiller flat

The tiller flat, also called the lazarette, is the aftmost space on the boat. Here the steering gear is fixed to the rudders and the exhausts exit through the transom. It often

ABOVE A panorama of the engine room taken from the forward bulkhead at frame 42, looking aft. To the left of the picture (the starboard side of the boat) is the access ladder into the wheelhouse and behind it the large red fire extinguisher, which can be activated in the engine room or from the bridge. Aft of the central engine is the deck access ladder and behind that sits the auxiliary engine. To the right of the picture (port side) the steering linkages can be seen running along the deckhead. Large beams support the weight of the Oerlikon turret above and the blue pipes lead from the air vents on deck to the bilge. *(Author)*

functions as a store, although it's important to make sure that items left here do not snag the steering mechanism or are left alongside the exhausts.

LEFT Looking forward at the centre engine with the bulkhead at frame 42 in the background. *(Author)*

Chapter Four

The MGB at war

The MGB's main role was to counter enemy S-boats, but it took time, practice, technological improvements and a resistance to Admiralty indifference for this to happen. When the Mk V came into service, all the necessary pieces fell into place and the tables turned in the waters around Great Britain.

OPPOSITE MTB 457. Originally ordered as MGB 138, she was the last Mk V to be built. (Al Ross)

ABOVE MGB 16, a 70ft British Power Boat, and MGB 100, a 69ft Higgins example. The star on MGB 16's bow suggests this photograph was taken around the time of D-Day, when the star was used as an identification symbol on Allied boats. (Peter Scott)

BELOW A German publicity photograph of S 19 with the pennant number crudely obscured. S 19 was an early-model S-boat that operated in the North Sea with the 1st Flotilla in the initial years of the war. (Author's Collection)

Trials and tribulations

As new boats came off the slips at the British Power Boat yard at Hythe they were hastily formed into MA/SB flotillas. In January 1941 these were redesignated MGB flotillas and the boats, while keeping their pennant numbers, swapped their initials from MA/SB to MGB. By the spring of 1941 seven flotillas were operational or forming up, utilising a mix of British Power Boat 63ft and 70ft boats and Lend-Lease boats from the USA, including some early PT boat designs from Higgins and 12 from Elco. Elco's boats were in fact almost identical to the British Power Boats, having been built to Scott-Paine's design when he arrived in the USA.

But things did not begin too happily for the early flotillas. The boats themselves were unreliable – the hulls had not been designed for the strain of the extra horsepower or the weight of weapons. Failures were frequent and boats were more often than not out of service undergoing maintenance.

A more serious problem was that no one had really given any thought about how best to employ MGBs. The flotillas were sent to bases and the local command was left to employ them as they saw fit, but they had no more experience of utilising the boats than their crews did. Many flotillas were left kicking their heels while their local commanders tried to find ways to use them.

On the east coast, where the growing flotillas of S-boats were regularly striking at coastal convoys, any boat that could help defend merchant ships was needed. Soon experiments were under way to see how best to make use of the MGBs. At HMS *Beehive* in Felixstowe, Lieutenant Robert Hichens RNVR had recently arrived with MGB 64 to join the 6th MGB Flotilla. He recalled their early work was to patrol along the seaward flanks of convoys, operating with two destroyers, one ahead and one astern of a pair of MGBs. The idea was that the larger destroyers, using their RDF gear, would detect approaching S-boats and despatch the MGBs to intercept. The theory was sound enough and would actually become the basis of future cooperative patrols in 1944, but requiring the MGBs to maintain station between two destroyers was impossible. The rough seas that destroyers could cope with nearly dwarfed the smaller boats in their wake and the risk of being rammed by the larger ships was extremely high.

Later experiments involved sending the boats out at night with ASDIC-equipped trawlers to wait in areas where S-boats might be encountered. Others maintained constant patrols along set areas of coast, but this increased wear on the boats and highlighted another serious problem: the early MGBs made an absolute racket. Commanders could barely hear themselves speak, let alone hear enemy vessels approaching; they, conversely, would receive plenty of warning about the approach of the MGBs! Unsurprisingly there were few brushes with the enemy in early 1941 – Hichens saw his first S-boats in April, but in a matter of seconds they had sped out of sight into the darkness and although the MGB pursued the German boats for nearly half an hour, the brief action ended without result. Even then, Hichens didn't think much of his chances of engaging the enemy with the weapons fitted

to his boat. Although their Vickers machine guns were briefly bolstered by the acquisition of some Oerlikon 20mm guns, these were quickly reallocated to the Mediterranean.

The Admiralty could see little worth in these small boats. More powerful vessels were needed to engage S-boats and, in their opinion, this meant they needed to be larger. By the summer of June 1941, they believed they had found the solution.

Fairmile Marine

Fairmile Marine was founded by Noel Macklin in 1939. Taking his cue from the Elco motor launches of the First World War, Macklin believed that a fleet of small vessels suitable for patrol, minelaying and minesweeping, could be created using prefabricated boats. The method was simple: component parts of motor launches were constructed at the company HQ in Cobham, Surrey, transported to boat yards around the country in kit form and assembled into complete boats. The first design for a 110ft launch designed by Norman Hart (later designated the Fairmile A), was not an ideal boat, but its method of construction was. The Admiralty had an existing design completed just before the war by Sydney Graham who became head of Fairmile's design office. Soon boat yards were busy producing hundreds of examples of the new Fairmile B. Officially designated motor launches (MLs) the boats became maids of all work, chiefly employed as patrol, escort, rescue, minelaying and minesweeping boats. However, although at 112ft they had the size to carry more firepower to tackle enemy S-boats, their two Hall Scott Defender engines did not give them the speed necessary to engage them.

In 1939, William Holt, then the head of the small boat section of the Department of Naval Construction, designed a 115ft hull that married the sharp bow of a destroyer to the rear end of a fast motorboat. Sufficiently large to accommodate four powerful engines, this boat could have the size and speed to challenge the S-boat and was perfect for production by Fairmile Marine. While designs for the new boat were perfected in 1940, the Admiralty sought

RIGHT A Fairmile B
motor launch. (Author's
Collection)

a temporary solution. Using the building jigs for the Fairmile A and equipping the boats with three Hall Scott engines, a new gun boat was quickly created. Designated the Fairmile C, the first boats were completed in June 1941, just as the keel of the first of the new Holt-designed boats was being laid. Equipped as MGBs, 24 Fairmile Cs were built in 1941, providing three much-needed flotillas.

With the Fairmile Cs being built in 13 boat yards around the country and Holt's design beginning to take shape, the Admiralty considered that the future of the MGB lay in 'long' boats and that the 'short' British Power

BELOW A Fairmile C
MGB. (Peter Scott)

Boats would soon be superseded. The order for 24 of Selman's new design was cut to eight in March 1941. Once the long boats were in service, they would no longer be needed.

Into action

Despite all their problems, by late 1941, the crews of the 70ft MGBs were getting to grips with their work. At the 6th Flotilla, scrounging had procured some better armament and several boats were now equipped with 0.5in machine guns and 20mm Oerlikon cannon. This still wasn't enough to destroy an S-boat, though, and the MGBs also carried a pair of depth charges that might be able to sink targets. A method of reducing the engine noise was found by fitting S-pipes – curving pipes extending from the exhaust down to sea level where traps could be used to close the exhaust for short periods. They weren't silencers, but they improved matters.

Robert Hichens had been promoted to lieutenant commander and became the senior officer of the flotilla in the late summer. Building on the crews' experience throughout the year, he began to explore the best way to engage S-boats. Finding them in the North Sea at night would always be difficult, but one place they were guaranteed to be found was outside their

ABOVE MGB 16 follows a 70ft MGB at sea. *(Peter Scott)*

LEFT An S 38-class S-boat at sea. By 1941 these were the most common S-boats encountered in home waters. *(BMPT Collection, via PNBPT)*

own bases. Patrols began to cross the North Sea once darkness fell to wait off the Dutch coast, hoping to intercept the S-boats on their return from a night's patrol.

On the night of 19 November 1941, Hichens led three boats to patrol along the Dutch coast. As had become typical by now, one of the boats broke down before they had proceeded more than a few miles from the English coast and had to return to base. Shortly after, one of the engines in MGB 64, Hichens' own boat, developed a fault and he had to reduce speed. Instead of going to the Dutch coast, 64 and 67 sailed into the middle of the North Sea and decided to lie in wait there.

Monitoring radio chatter from the coastal convoys, Hichens worked out roughly where S-boats had made attacks that night and plotted their most likely routes back to their bases. After sailing to a position where they might intercept, the MGBs cut their motors and waited, listening for the sound of engines carrying across the sea.

Just before 5:00am on 20 November, through strained ears, the crews heard the low rumble of diesel engines. That night 11 boats of the 2nd and 4th S-boat Flotillas had

attacked convoy FS 650, sinking three large merchant ships. During the attack S 41 and S 47 collided, causing such damage to both that they had to be towed. Now, one group of five boats, including the lame S 41, was approaching Hichens' position.

Listening carefully and estimating the noise's course, the two gun boats repositioned to intercept. A few minutes later, in the gloom ahead of them, the crews suddenly spotted the five S-boats rendezvousing at slow speed. The two MGBs had caught the S-boats unawares and immediately attacked, firing into the mass of startled German vessels, which quickly scattered. As the MGBs prowled further into the darkness they met a single enemy boat and poured merciless gunfire into its hull, before it too escaped into the gloom.

As the British crews searched further, to their surprise they came across another boat lying stopped in the water. Hichens sent MGB 67 forward to depth charge the boat and disable it, but it quickly became apparent that the enemy vessel wasn't going anywhere. S 41, already badly damaged in the earlier collision, had been abandoned by the Germans, and her crew taken off on to one of the other boats which, even now, were beating a hasty retreat to Rotterdam. They would later report that they had been attacked by up to 14 gun boats and perhaps this had hastened them to escape before confirming that S 41 was properly scuttled.

The MGBs cautiously approached the abandoned vessel and boarded her. Hurriedly the British crews stripped the S-boat of anything of value. Hichens hoped to take her in tow back to England, but it was quickly apparent that she was sinking. Even if the scuttling hadn't been completely effective, the depth charge attack had finished her off. Less than an hour later she slipped beneath the waves. As soon as she was gone, the MGBs turned for home and in the light of the morning sailed into Felixstowe with the S-boat's Kriegsmarine flag fluttering below the White Ensign on MGB 64's mast.

New tactics and new boats

Further south at Dover, the 3rd MGB Flotilla under Lieutenant Stewart Gould was also achieving success. Working with the 6th MTB Flotilla, the crews attacked enemy convoys together. The MGBs brought much-needed firepower to support the Vosper MTBs (which were only equipped with one twin Vickers gun turret) and could help distract escorts while the MTBs sneaked in close enough to make their torpedo attacks. On the night of 3/4 November 1941, MGBs 42 and 43 accompanied MTBs 38, 218 and 220 to attack a convoy off Cap Gris-Nez on the French coast. The two MGBs bravely roared in first and took on a large German M-class minesweeper and a T-class torpedo boat (more akin to a small destroyer than an MTB), both scoring hits on the larger German vessels. They sustained serious damage in return, but their work enabled the MTBs to make an attack on the 5,000-ton merchant ship *Batavier V* and send her to the bottom.

Hichens' success in November 1941 was quickly followed by another encounter in December, but winter brought with it ever-worsening weather and this began to affect the operations of the short boats. Planing hulls are designed to lift out of the water and skim, so in rough seas the boat tends to slam into waves. In high seas it's impossible for them to manoeuvre, much less fight, and many patrols were scrubbed due to the weather.

BELOW Fairmile D MGB 664, one of the new class of 'long' MGBs. *(Crown Copyright)*

Instead, the newly completed Fairmile Cs became the main line of defence. Their longer, round bilge hulls were better able to cope with the weather and in February 1942, boats of the 16th MGB Flotilla, along with destroyers and motor launches escorting a convoy, engaged S-boats in the North Sea. One of the S-boats was so badly damaged that it was scuttled by its crew.

In October 1941, the first of the new Fairmiles designed by Holt had been launched. Designated a Fairmile D, the 115ft boat immediately began trials to perfect the design. Bristling with armament and able to sail in rough seas, the Admiralty were very happy with the boat and by the time the prototype entered service as MGB 601 in March 1942, another 99 boats had been ordered. Eventually 206 were built, of which 50 were completed as MGBs. It was soon realised that they were capable of carrying torpedoes and retaining heavy guns, so the rest were completed as MTBs.

The Fairmile D was an incredibly successful boat and several flotillas even sailed to the Mediterranean where they did sterling service. But at an absolute maximum speed of 34kts,

they were too slow to run down S-boats. Hichens' success in the North Sea led the Admiralty to reconsider the future of the short boats and, in February 1942, the order for one of the British Power Boat flotillas cancelled a year previously was reinstated, followed by the other in April.

Spring brought with it a return to regular operations. The Fairmile Cs were well suited to patrol work and freed up the short boats to hunt for S-boats. On the night of 14/15 March 1942, three boats of the 7th MGB Flotilla, under the command of Lieutenant Bremer Horne, lay in wait off the Dutch coast. It was starting to get light and the MGBs prepared to sail for home when S 111 of the 2nd S-boat Flotilla hove into view. A short, sharp action followed, and the S-boat was forced to surrender. The British quickly prepared to tow her back to England, but a few hours later, in the middle of the North Sea, three more S-boats intercepted them, intent on recapturing their sister vessel. The British were forced to abandon their prize and escape to the west, while the Germans began to tow the crippled boat back to IJmuiden in the Netherlands. Fortunately, alerted by the MGBs, a squadron

OPPOSITE A Fairmile C pounds into heavy weather. *(Peter Scott)*

BELOW Royal Navy MGB crews pore over the luckless S 111. *(IWM A10820)*

ABOVE **MGB 116, one of the early Mk V MGBs.**
(CFHT Collection)

of Spitfires found the S-boats a few hours later and sank the luckless S 111.

The short MGBs began to sail every night in the hope of intercepting S-boats. On the evening of 21 April 1942, Hichens tried a new tactic and took four boats across the North Sea in daylight. At dusk they arrived off the Belgian coast near Ostend, hoping to catch S-boats as they set out on their raids of the English coast. They were rewarded when six S-boats appeared out of the harbour and instantly the MGBs pounced. A ferocious battle erupted as the MGBs closed station on a parallel course, running alongside the S-boats before they could accelerate away. In a battle more akin to the days when great wooden Men O'War fired broadsides on each other, both sides poured gunfire into one another until the Germans broke off the engagement. As the MGB crews treated their wounded, the S-boat engines could be heard retreating back into harbour. Hichens remained off the coast until the early hours of the next morning, but the Germans did not attempt to leave the harbour again that night. The short battle marked a turning point in the MGBs' war. Not only had

the gun boats prevented the S-boats from intercepting a convoy, they had done so right on the enemy-held coast, rather than Britain's.

A purpose-built MGB

By now the MGB crews were making contact with the S-boats with greater regularity, and combined MTB and MGB operations off the enemy's coast were yielding more results. In early 1942, Hichens had got wind of the new British Power Boat MGBs, the first of which were nearing completion. Many of his commanders were sceptical about the design, especially the 2-pounder pom-pom, which they believed was mounted too far forward and would not be useable on a bouncing vessel. The real future of MGBs was still felt to be with the Fairmile Ds. Hichens disagreed entirely, knowing that a forward-facing 40mm gun would not only be devastatingly effective in combat, but that forward of the bridge was the best (and driest) place to put it. Upon making enquiries, he found that the boats were to be allocated to the next set of crews to become available, but Hichens felt strongly that his experienced flotilla would be able to make better use of them. He agitated long and hard to get the eight boats sent to him and finally the Admiralty relented.

In February 1942 the first of the new Mk V boats, MGB 74, was commissioned and two months later it arrived at Felixstowe. Hichens' crews were delighted – finally they had a small, fast boat with armament capable of doing real damage to S-boats. The three Packard engines were fast and, more importantly, reliable. The bridge was fitted with a small amount of armour plating to protect the crews and a basic but effective RDF set was fitted, affording the chance to detect enemy vessels for themselves. In the early summer, Hichens investigated ways of silencing his boat's engines. After experimenting with underwater exhausts, he met with Selman who commented later:

> Hichens persisted and at last I said I would put them through the bottom of the ruddy boat somehow. However, he was not satisfied until I there and then sketched out an arrangement. I must say that the result surprised even Hitch because we obtained a nearly silent exhaust, very low back pressure only one quarter of a pound above open exhaust and, in addition added three knots to the speed of the boat.[1]

Meanwhile, a new defence against S-boats had been established on the east coast. In the summer of 1942 the Z line was introduced. It consisted of 35 mooring buoys in two lines seaward of the convoy routes, just inside the defensive minefield off the coast of East Anglia. The outer line of 26 buoys were moored every 4 miles, with a sparser line of 9 buoys 10 miles behind them, each given their own code number prefixed by Z. On any given night approximately one-third of the buoys would be occupied by a unit of two or more Coastal Forces boats – usually MGBs, Fairmile Ds or MLs. The system made it easier to defend the convoy route and left the S-boats guessing where the defending boats might be waiting.

---

1 Selman, 2000, p. 8.

War in the Channel

By now the S-boats were facing greater threats than just the MGBs. More heavily armed destroyers were available for convoy escort duty and the RAF was slowly gaining air superiority. The arrival of Coastal Forces boats equipped with RDF also made interceptions easier, and the German vessels had no equivalent.

At the beginning of June 1942, the 2nd and 4th S-boat Flotillas relocated from their bases on the Dutch and Belgian coasts to Boulogne and, at the end of the month, to Cherbourg. The switch from operations in the North Sea to the English Channel was partly precipitated by the shorter summer nights that reduced the effective time that the boats could operate. Crossing the North Sea took time, while Cherbourg was significantly closer to the Channel's east–west convoy routes. But at the same time, there was a recognition of a distinct turn of the tide in the North Sea – torpedo attacks against east-coast convoys had become less and less successful, largely as a result of the interference of the Royal Navy's MGBs. It was hoped that the Channel would provide fresh hunting grounds.

The intention was to attack the convoys

BELOW The forward 20mm gun on an S-boat. (*Bundesarchiv Bild 101II-MW-6304-13A*)

sailing along England's south coast using a new tactic, the *stichansatz* or 'stab'. Basing their approach on intelligence reports, an S-boat formation would sail north towards a dead-reckoned position to meet the convoy. Some 10–15 miles south of the position, the S-boats would fan out and, in pairs separated by a gap of approximately 2 miles, lie in wait along the anticipated convoy line.

The tactic relied on good intelligence, good position-keeping and, ideally, regular air reconnaissance to maintain contact with the convoy. Bad weather plagued the S-boats at the start of July, but on the night of 8/9 July, Convoy WP 183, sailing from Milford Haven to Portsmouth, was intercepted by eight S-boats of the 2nd Flotilla in Lyme Bay. No radar contacts were picked up by the *Hunt*-class destroyer HMS *Brocklesby* on escort duty and the first sign of an attack was when a torpedo slammed into the side of the anti-submarine escort trawler HMT *Manor*. Each group of S-boats made their attacks on the convoy, sinking five merchant ships totalling 12,182 gross tonnes.

The stab was a significant and morale-boosting success for the two flotillas, although they would not repeat it in the Channel again that year. Another attempt in August, pitting 16 S-boats against convoy PW 196, failed to sink any merchant ships. Nonetheless, the attack on WP 183 stung the Royal Navy into reinforcing the south coast. With five of the new Mk V gun boats now operational at HMS *Beehive*, Hichens formed the new 8th MGB Flotilla. Almost immediately he received the order to transfer to HMS *Cicala* at Dartmouth.[2] Departing Felixstowe early on 12 July, the five boats of the flotilla reached Dartmouth the same evening – a journey of around 260nm.

Hichens was ready to patrol that same night, although Dartmouth was far from ready for them and their first patrol was made on the night of 14/15 July. That night three of the new boats found and shot up two enemy trawlers north of Alderney, even crossing the bows of one to drop a depth charge. The value of the armoured bridge showed itself when

a 40mm shell hit the wheelhouse, knocking out power to the turrets, starting a fire and killing a member of Hichens' crew. Despite the damage, the crew on the bridge were unharmed. It had been a blooding for the new boats, but on the other hand, they left two ruined armed enemy trawlers behind them.

On the night of 1/2 August, Hichens led four of his boats to seek out S-boats heading for the English coast. A few hours later he received signals from shore stations and vessels that had spotted S-boats at sea and moved to intercept them as they returned to Cherbourg. Arriving at the breakwater, the German shore stations appeared oblivious to their presence and Hichens found himself within 700m of a German torpedo boat (a small destroyer). It was too large for them to tackle with guns alone – had Hichens had an MTB with him, she would have been an easy target.

Instead the MGBs focused their attention on a returning patrol of what may have been S-boats or slightly smaller minelaying R-boats (*Räumboote*). Assuming they were safely home from their patrol, the German crews' attention was lax and the MGBs stole up to the end of the line of enemy boats. At near point-blank range, the MGBs opened fire, instigating a cacophony of gunfire as confused German vessels, the torpedo boat and even shore batteries fired wildly into the night. For 12 minutes the MGBs pounded the German flotilla and then withdrew, leaving a confused enemy continuing the battle among themselves. The glow of the fires behind them were still visible when the MGBs were 4 miles away.

The action had been an incredible success, but it sparked in Hichens a new idea. With torpedoes, they could have done even more damage and the new boats, he reasoned, could probably be adapted to carry at least one. He was already aware that they were heavier than necessary owing to the weighty power-operated turrets and the excess ammunition they were obliged to carry. From this moment on, Hichens began to lobby for a change in his new boat's armament.

In August the S-boats returned to the North Sea and the 8th MGB Flotilla followed them.

2   Most memoirs and even the Admiralty movement orders refer to Dartmouth, although the Coastal Forces' main HQ was the requisitioned Royal Dart Hotel in Kingswear on the other side of the river.

For the rest of the year and over the winter, both sides played their deadly game of cat and mouse, the S-boats attempting to sneak past the patrols off the Dutch coast and through the Z line, the MGBs trying to catch them unawares. The S-boats still had teeth, though. On the night of 10/11 September, four Fairmile Cs intercepted a group of S-boats returning to the Dutch coast but quickly discovered they were outnumbered and outgunned. No fewer than nine S-boats joined the fray and in the battle that followed MGB 335 was crippled and had to be abandoned. Her crew were taken off and the boat was fired upon by her fellow Fairmiles to sink it before they withdrew. The British thought she was finished, but the following morning she was towed into a Dutch port by the S-boats, complete with charts of British minefields, signal books and a working RDF set. The Kriegsmarine were able to keep their prize secret until the end of the war, scoring a valuable intelligence victory over the Royal Navy. On the night of 2/3 October, the

Mk V MGBs suffered their first loss when MGB 78 was destroyed (see Chapter 6). Hichens himself had a lucky escape on 5/6 October when MGB 76 was set ablaze in an action with S-boats and the crew had to abandon ship. Fortunately, they were picked up in the morning, but 76 was the second Mk V MGB to be lost in three nights.

At the same time, the MGBs were making an impact against enemy vessels other than the S-boats. MTB crews were continuing to evolve the best methods to attack enemy coastal convoys off the coast of Europe. Officers such as Lieutenant Peter Dickens, in command of the 21st MTB Flotilla, continued to build on the successful work of the previous year, evolving elaborate tactics to combine the weight of firepower of an MGB with the destructive capabilities of their torpedo boats. By 1943 they were enjoying such success that the Kriegsmarine even began sailing some convoys by day in an effort to avoid the MTBs, but this only made them targets for the RAF.

ABOVE Another frequent target in the Channel were *Räumboote* or R-boats. Similar in size to S-boats, these vessels were usually equipped for minelaying or sweeping and lacked torpedo tubes. *(CFHT Collection)*

'Spitfires of the Sea' is an apt moniker for the MGBs and MTBs of Coastal Forces, but the first time the phrase was used in print was actually to describe an aircraft. In November and December 1940, articles extolling Royal Navy aircraft of the Fleet Air Arm, including the Blackburn Skua and the Fairey Fulmar, appeared in regional newspapers in Britain. Titled 'The Spitfires of the Sea', the similarities in some of these articles suggests they may have originated from an Admiralty press release, perhaps attempting to compare the aircraft to their more famous namesake that had so recently captured the public's attention in the Battle of Britain.

Nonetheless, in 1941 and 1942, newspapers began to link the phrase to Coastal Forces. An article in the *Manchester Evening News* in June 1941 made reference to the 'Big Rush to Be in Sea "Spitfire" Service', and in September 1942, an article in the *Daily Herald* on the Women's Royal Naval Service contribution to the small boat war was entitled 'The Spanner Girls Keep Our Sea-Spitfires Fighting'.

In August 1942, well-known naval correspondent for the *Daily Herald* A.J. McWhinnie penned an article in which he stated 'Our Coastal Forces are the Spitfires of the sea, manned by youngsters. Thirty is old in this service.' From then on, the phrase became well established and in 1943 it even appeared in newspapers as far away as Australia.

In October 1943 the book *Little Ships*, by journalist Gordon Holman, was published. Holman was well known in Coastal Forces – he had accompanied the St Nazaire Raid on the bridge of a Fairmile C in 1942. When describing the armament commonly found on MGBs, Holman observed that 'When all these are firing in close action from a little vessel of about a hundred feet in length it can be well understood why the gunboats have been called the "Spitfires of the sea".' Holman's is perhaps the only attempt to link MGBs specifically to the phrase – in the main it was applied to both MTBs and MGBs in the press. In 1945 Lieutenant Commander Peter Scott, son of the Antarctic explorer Robert Falcon Scott and a senior figure in Coastal Forces, had his book, *The Battle of the Narrow Seas*, published. In it he states: 'The tracer bullets and the flying spray, the torpedo attacks and the high-speed gun battles – these are the spectacular aspects of Coastal Forces, the Spitfires of the sea.' Importantly, though, he goes on to remind the reader that 'in the Channel and North Sea they made up much less than one-tenth of the work of our light craft'. It is true that while the glamour and epithets are well associated with MGBs and MTBs, the Fairmile MLs and HDMLs are sadly far less well remembered.

Changing roles

Hichens firmly believed that the rear power-operated twin Oerlikon turret on his Mk V boats could be replaced with a hand-trained mounting. The power-operated turrets were vulnerable to enemy fire – a single bullet could damage the power supply and leave the turret fixed in one direction and therefore completely useless. Hichens judged that a well-designed hand-trained mounting could support the weight of two Oerlikons, which would have the additional benefit of reducing the boat's weight and even making it possible to fit torpedo tubes. The Admiralty demurred, believing that torpedoes were unnecessary and that twin Oerlikons would be too heavy to operate by hand. Exasperated by the Admiralty's unflinching ignorance of operational experience, the 8th MGB Flotilla began experimenting for themselves. *Beehive*'s Gunnery Officer, Lieutenant Woods, created a simple gun mount that allowed two Oerlikons to be fitted on to the cradle of a single hand-operated Oerlikon mount. The prototype was installed on MGB 79 and soon several more boats were sporting an additional Oerlikon or two on their sterns.

Throughout the winter of 1942/43, the Mk V MGBs (of which there were now two flotillas) encountered targets that would have been easily despatched with a torpedo, but which were largely invulnerable to gunfire. Hichens related his thoughts to George Selman and the designer put forward five potential modifications to the MGBs that would reduce their weight and allow torpedo tubes to be fitted. MGB 77 was experimentally equipped with a pair of torpedo tubes and, on 25 February, Hichens joined Selman to inspect MGB 123 at Hythe. British Power Boat had modified the boat by fitting a set of the customised hand-trained Oerlikons developed at HMS *Beehive*.

Still the Admiralty were unconvinced. The MGB's purpose they decreed, was to intercept

OPPOSITE A hand-trained twin Oerlikon mount designed by Lieutenant Woods at HMS *Beehive*. MGB 81 can be seen in the background.
(IWM A14552)

ABOVE MGB 123 became the prototype Mk VI 71ft 6in boat, which heralded the end of the MGB. *(Southampton City Heritage Services)*

BELOW MTB 447 at sea. Originally ordered as MGB 128, she was the first of the Mk V boats to be commissioned as an MTB, but did not receive torpedo tubes. *(Christopher Timms)*

S-boats, not torpedo them. The hand-trained Oerlikons, they argued, would be too heavy for crewmen to use, ignoring the fact that Hichens' flotilla had been using Woods' design for several months.

Slowly, however, changes began to be made. By April steps were being taken to investigate a combined MTB and MGB and, in the summer, British Power Boat further modified MGB 123 by fitting torpedo tubes and a short wheelhouse (or MTB-type bridge) to create more room to load the tubes.

Unfortunately, these changes came too late for Hichens. On the night of 12/13 April, he sailed on MGB 112, along with MGBs 74, 75 and 111, accompanying a flotilla of Fairmile motor launches laying a minefield off the Dutch coast. Once completed, the gun boats continued to patrol the coast and soon came across two armed trawlers. Engaging the largest of the two, the MGBs were just turning away when a single cannon shell hit MGB 112's bridge, killing Hichens instantly and wounding three others.

Hichens' death sent shockwaves through the Coastal Forces community and much of the British public, who had read of his exploits in the press and heard tales of his actions on the wireless. The following month, another notable officer, George Richards, commander of the 9th MGB Flotilla, was killed off Dunkirk. Surprised by six S-boats, Richards had just signalled Nelson's famous command 'Engage the enemy more closely', when his boat was hit at point-blank range and destroyed.

The end of the MGB

In August 1943 the Admiralty concluded that in future, all British Power Boat's new MGBs would be finished as MTBs. Starting with the boats nearing completion at Hythe, Selman's design for a hand-trained Oerlikon mounting would replace the power-operated turret. MGB 128 was the first boat to be launched as an MTB (447), although not all of the boats were actually equipped with torpedo tubes. However, British Power Boat's experiments with MGB 123 led to the development of the Mk VI boat and, by the following spring, new boats were completed as true MTBs, with short wheelhouses and torpedoes as standard.

On 26 August 1943, an official order from the Admiralty issued to local commands announced the reclassification of the existing flotillas of Mk V MGBs to MTBs. Over the following weeks, the 8th, 9th and 10th MGB Flotillas became the 1st, 2nd and 3rd MTB Flotillas, replacing the original MTB units that had been disbanded the previous year when their boats became obsolete.

Short MGBs still survived in the form of the 70ft British Power Boats, and Fairmile D MGBs were still active in the Mediterranean, but essentially the short MTBs and MGBs had evolved into heavily armed fast patrol boats, capable of fulfilling either role. In January 1944, Vosper's new Type I 73ft MTB was launched, a boat capable of carrying four 18in torpedoes. By the end of the war the design was being constructed as the Type II and, like the British Power Boats, combined the benefits of two torpedo tubes with the advantages of heavy weaponry.

The change did not introduce torpedo tubes to every British Power Boat. Many of the boats already in service did not change at all – some had their rear turret modified to the hand-trained mounting but otherwise their role as MGBs remained unchanged. In the original flotillas, perhaps one or two boats were equipped with torpedoes so that mixed

ABOVE MTB 387, a Vosper Type I 73ft MTB, equipped with four 18in torpedoes. *(CFHT Collection)*

BELOW MTB 530, a Type II 73ft MTB. Although her construction began in 1944, MTB 530 was not completed until after the war. *(BMPT Collection via PNBPT)*

ABOVE MTB 449, ordered as a Mk V MGB, was completed and commissioned as a Mk V MTB in September 1943. *(CFHT Collection)*

formations from the same unit could patrol together, maintaining the firepower of the MGBs with the valuable option of MTBs if they were needed.

By now, improvements in technology were also influencing the flotillas' tactics. Operating from a shore-based radar station, a naval controller scanned the sea for enemy vessels. Once an enemy target was identified, the controller could vector Coastal Forces boats on an intercept course using radio phone (radio transmitters) instead of telegraphy. Once close enough, the MTBs could pick up the enemy vessels with their own RDF and close to visual range. The system was highly effective and increased the interceptions of S-boats after the first successful operation in April 1944.

In the meantime, the original Mk V boats kept up their offensive actions on the enemy coast. Desperate to obtain useful intelligence, the S-boats planned to capture a boat and, on 14/15 February, the 2nd and 8th S-boat Flotillas set out from the Dutch coast. Meanwhile, four boats of the 3rd MTB Flotilla

(still equipped with standard Mk V MGBs), accompanied by the torpedo-equipped Mk V MTB 455 of the 4th Flotilla, had begun a patrol off IJmuiden on the Dutch coast, where they encountered enemy trawlers and a flak ship. MTB 455 quickly made a successful attack on a trawler while the four MGBs drew fire, but suddenly another flak ship poured fire on to them, striking MTB 444 and mortally wounding the flotilla's senior officer. While 444 limped home, the other three boats reduced the flak ship to a blazing hulk until, moments later, the 2nd and 8th S-boat Flotillas arrived on the scene. Although they were outnumbered four to one, the British crews made several attacks on the lines of S-boats attempting to reach their port, only withdrawing at 4:40am. The Germans failed to obtain a gun boat that night.

Neptune

All thoughts now turned to the long-awaited invasion of Europe. While offensive patrols in the North Sea continued, more flotillas were directed south to the Channel to harry the S-boats there and take control of 'Britain's Moat'.

An obvious extension of the shore-based naval controller was to place them in ships with suitable RDF equipment. This way, the successful interception system could be carried to the other side of the Channel. In April, the flotillas that were to be involved in Operation Neptune were assigned to control frigates. On board each frigate was a naval controller, a Coastal Forces officer with experience on MTBs or MGBs, to monitor the seas around the invasion fleet with radar and vector the MTBs accordingly. In guarding the fleet against the anticipated threat of S-boats, MGBs would once again be a valuable weapon and many of the unconverted MTBs were assigned to the invasion fleet.

The other threat to the invasion force was the underwater enemy. Knowing that U-boats would quickly arrive on the scene and with concern mounting about intelligence reports of midget submarines operating from German bases, the decision was made to equip some Mk V and Mk VI boats with rudimentary racks capable of holding up to 48 small Mk XII depth charges filled with the explosive Minol.

In some instances, this led to the unhappy development that Mk VI boats had their torpedo tubes removed. The 29th (Canadian) MTB Flotilla were still working up at Holyhead when they received the news that they were to lose their torpedoes and instead receive depth charges. The unit had been training as MTBs and to be deprived of what they felt was their most important weapon was a bitter blow to the crews. In fact the British Power Boats had come full circle. The MTBs were operating in essentially the same role as their MA/SB predecessor, but with the full armament of an MGB.

When D-Day came, the boats of Coastal Forces were at the forefront. Fairmile B minesweepers sailed ahead of the fleet sweepers at the head of the huge task forces sailing to each beach, while Harbour Defence Motor Launches acted as navigation leaders. Vospers, British Power Boats and Dog Boats patrolled the flanks of the convoys while control frigates searched for S-boats to vector roving patrols on to.

Following the main landings, the flotillas and their control frigates kept up their guard duties constantly, intercepting S-boats, U-boats and midget submarines night after night. On board one of the control frigates – HMS *Stayner* – Lieutenant Ian Menzies witnessed at first hand

BELOW MTB 459 was commissioned in March 1944 and served with the 29th (Canadian) MTB Flotilla at Normandy. *(BMPT Collection via PNBPT)*

ABOVE **MTB 451 of the 35th MTB Flotilla, based at HMS *Hornet* during Operation Neptune. On the night of 7 July, the flotilla's senior officer was killed on 451's bridge while engaging S-boats.**
(Christopher Timms)

the impact of the close-quarters action the MTBs were involved in.

One has to picture first, one of those close-fought actions. An MTB has made a daring torpedo attack on an F lighter. She had come under concentrated fire from at least three German boats at point blank range. The torpedo had struck its target, and the MTB had moved to seaward. She had sent a message to us requesting to transfer casualties. The doctor who we carried on every trip was notified. I had arranged a rapid system of hospitalization whereby stretchers were slid on specially constructed trestles, down from the upper deck to a large seamen's mess-deck below. Here the doctor, sick berth attendant and medical party got on with their jobs.

I was standing on the deck and could hear the heavy roar of the MTB drawing closer. The darkness of the night was intense. The stretcher party and I had shielded flashlights ready. When I saw the sharp flat bows of the MTB about 20 yards from the ship, I flashed my light once or twice to indicate where I wanted her to come alongside. There was a slow, sluggish swell. The boat rolled gently as she nosed her way alongside, her engine ticking over slowly. Ropes were thrown and she was secured alongside. In the darkness, broken only by the occasional flicker of a flashlight, it was a spectral scene.

The deck of the MTB was a mess of ropes, discarded clothing and empty cartridge cases. On the deck men were lying silently. One or two seamen were talking to them – going from one to another, adjusting a blanket here a bandage there, whispering 'It's all right Bill.'

The captain leaned wearily from his 'dust bin cockpit'. There was blood on his face. The engines were still ticking over.

'We'll take over now!' I yelled above the noise.

He answered quietly, dazedly. 'Ok. We had a pretty rough time.'

Our stretcher party went on board. I heard one man groan faintly as with a shattered leg he was placed on a stretcher. The men on the boat moved about slowly. They said little. Over all was the smell of exhaust fumes and burning cordite. The deck was slippery with petrol, water and blood.

The 1st lieutenant of the MTB spoke to a rating telling him to board Stayner. The man had a bandaged arm and his trouser leg was ripped. He was limping. He replied that he would stay, that he was all right. I asked the captain of the boat if he had been hit. He looked in bad shape. Lee had come down from the bridge and was asking him questions about the action. One more rating was brought up from the engine room. The clothing over his chest was torn. I was amazed there was so little blood. It was just a deep, raw and jagged wound. He was the last to be transferred. We hustled them all below. It had all taken just over 10 minutes. The first lieutenant asked me if I had any more morphine as he had used his. I passed him over a complete box which I always carried.

'Just in case,' he added, 'thanks.'

They got ready to leave again. The deck was clearer now. Empty cartridge cases were still clanking about on the deck to each roll of the ship. The noise jangled on the nerves. The engines, which had never stopped, were revved up and the lines let go. She disappeared to be swallowed up in the darkness again – back onto patrol. That was one occasion. It happened many times.[3]

---

3   Menzies, 2012, pp. 148–51.

Towards the end

In August the Allied ground forces broke out of Normandy and resistance in France collapsed. German naval forces evacuated their bases and the brunt of the fighting returned to the North Sea. Despite their losses, the S-boats were still willing to take the fight to the enemy and attacks on east-coast convoys began again, although the high rate of interceptions curtailed most of their efforts. The MGBs returned to a routine of patrols on the Z line and offensive sweeps of the Dutch coast.

Once the Allies had liberated Antwerp, regular convoys began sailing from the Thames Estuary for the Scheldt, providing tempting targets for the S-boats. As the nights lengthened and the winter weather blew up, the boats of Coastal Forces fought regular actions with their counterparts. The rough seas soon forced the Dog Boats to take on most of the work, but there were some chances for the short boats to get into the fight. When

24 S-boats set out from Dutch ports to attack convoys sailing to Antwerp on the night of 22/23 January, Mk V and Mk VI boats of the 35th MTB Flotilla intercepted and drove them back, with the loss of only one merchant ship.

On the night of 6/7 April 1945, the S-boats scored their last success against Coastal Forces. Six boats of the 2nd Flotilla sailed from Den Helder to mine the approaches to the Humber Estuary. Around midnight they were attacked by destroyers off the British coast and, as they withdrew, by two Fairmile D MTBs. In a close-fought action, the S-boats were able to hit MTB 5001's engine room and she sank shortly after. The S-boats set course for home, now shadowed by RAF aircraft who were able to vector an MTB patrol towards them and, off the coast of Norfolk, three Mk VI MTBs of the 22nd MTB Flotilla moved into position to intercept.

MTBs 493, 494 and 497 had seen flashes on the horizon when the S-boats engaged the Fairmile Ds, but in the inky blackness, and unwilling to use their RDF lest it should alert

BELOW MTB 494, the last of the British Power Boats lost to enemy action.
(Author's Collection)

ABOVE MTBs 481 (Mk VI) and 454 (Mk V). MTB 454 was involved in the very last action between 'short' boats and German S-boats. *(Christopher Timms)*

RIGHT The damage to MTB 493, photographed by John Lake, her first lieutenant. *(John Lake Collection, via PNBPT)*

the German vessels to their presence, it was hard to spot the enemy boats. The S-boats had no radar of their own and were blind to the presence of the British Power Boats until it was too late. In the lead, MTB 494 saw the enemy first and roared into an attack, but as she opened fire on the German line, she was rammed by one of the S-boats and overturned.

MTB 493 now came into the melee when suddenly, in the darkness, S 197 appeared dead ahead and, with nowhere to go, the crew had no choice but to ram. As the two boats crashed into one another and ricocheted away, 493 fired into the S-boat at point-blank range, but as she picked up speed the MTB crashed fully into the upturned hull of 494.

ABOVE AND BELOW

A week after the action that almost destroyed MTB 493, the crew took over MTB 496.
(John Lake Collection, via PNBPT)

Two survivors from the capsized boat were rescued, while 497 took off S 197's crew and the luckless MTB 493, minus its bow, was towed stern-first into Lowestoft. Fifteen men and two Mk VI MTBs were lost (493 was never repaired), the last Coastal Forces casualties to the S-boats in the war.

The following night, two boats of the 35th MTB Flotilla fought the very last 'short' gun boat actions against S-boats. When boats of the 4th and 6th Flotillas sailed from Dutch ports that night, they were under constant observation by aircraft. MTBs 454 (Mk V) and 482 (Mk VI) were vectored towards one group of five S-boats by their control frigate HMS *Rutherford* and, once they had made contact, concentrated on S 202 and S 703 at the rear of the formation. The S-boats collided in the action and sank, the MTBs picking up 40 members of the crews.

It was the last time the short boats would meet the S-boats in action. The final S-boat operation in the North Sea was on 13 April, laying mines in the Scheldt Estuary before being forced to withdraw by Dog Boats. By now even operating at night was dangerous as combined air–sea cooperation had been perfected. Totally vulnerable from the air, outnumbered by Coastal Forces ten to one and short of fuel and ammunition, the S-boats' war ended almost a month before the forces on land surrendered, such was the domination of the Royal Navy.

The short boats had one final action off the Frisian Islands on 25/26 April, when Mk VI MTB 458, accompanied by four Vospers, engaged a convoy of vessels evacuating Dutch ports. A week later, Field Marshal Montgomery accepted the unconditional surrender of all German forces in Germany, Denmark and the Netherlands, bringing the fighting in the North Sea to an end. On VE Day, the scattered flotillas of Coastal Forces could finally breathe a welcome sigh of relief and relax. Sub

BELOW Two S 38b-class S-boats surrender to the Royal Navy at HMS *Beehive* in Felixstowe. *(Christopher Timms)*

Lieutenant Philip Seymour recalled that, as the Mk VI boats of the 30th MTB Flotilla sped home to Lowestoft, one of the boat skippers mischievously claimed to have received a signal from the Admiralty ordering crews to 'Splice the Main Brace', and liberal rations of rum were issued.

The next time the S-boats met the boats of Coastal Forces was when they were escorted into captivity. On 13 May, two S-boats entered Felixstowe dock to hand over charts of minefields and, in the following weeks, the remaining flotillas were directed to British ports around the coast.

Coastal Forces' victory was complete. The Royal Navy and the private boatbuilders of their fleet of 'Little Ships' had managed to evolve their boats to respond to the S-boat threat and the demands of the war. The evolution of the original MA/SBs into gun boats, followed by the introduction of purpose-built short and long MGBs along with the gradual improvements in weaponry, equipment such as hydrophones and RDF and, most importantly, tactics, enabled Coastal Forces to outclass their German counterparts. On the other side of the North Sea, the German Navy was never able to evolve its strategy to meet the rise of the MGB. The S-boats' mission was to intercept convoys and no thought was given to developing separate vessels to counter MGBs. Forced to fulfil both roles, the S-boats rarely succeeded in the latter and usually avoided directly engaging MGBs, even when the odds were in their favour. Likewise, German technology was unable to keep up with British developments; a radar was developed but never became standard equipment.

Once the MGBs had found the best tactics to engage their opponents, they became the hunters. As the MGBs evolved, the S-boats were forced on to the back foot and remained the hunted throughout the rest of the war.

BELOW German S-boats surrender at HMS *Hornet*, Portsmouth. In the background, left of the crane, is Boathouse 4, MGB 81's current home. *(IWM A29323)*

Chapter Five

Operating MGB 81

Even with modern aids on board, the principles and manner under which MGB 81 operates today are little changed from the 1940s. A ride on a genuine Coastal Forces vessel is an exhilarating experience, all the more so on a vessel of such age and significance.

OPPOSITE **MGB 81 under way in the Solent.** *(PNBPT)*

In 1942, MGBs were required nightly to patrol the seas around Britain, either on offensive missions on the enemy-held coast, or defensive patrols along the coastal convoy routes. The crews knew that if enemy vessels were at sea that night, they would need to be too. Today MGB 81, the last of her kind still able to put to sea, is not required to engage enemy warships and so the factor that most influences whether she sails or not is the ever-undependable British weather. Technically, MGB 81 is capable of sailing in the same rough waters that blighted the English Channel and North Sea in the 1940s – up to a Force 5 – but it is unlikely that she will put to sea in anything worse than a Force 3 sea today.

The person who will make that decision is Diggory Rose, Boatkeeper for the Portsmouth Naval Base Property Trust. Diggory is MGB 81's regular skipper and oversees the small crew of staff and volunteers from Boathouse 4, the Trust's exhibition space in Portsmouth Historic Dockyard.

Preparation

When it's decided that MGB 81 will put to sea, the first task is to prepare the engine room. If the bridge of a boat is the nerve centre, then the engine room is the heart: without its power supply, a motorboat isn't going anywhere.

The regular mechanic on board MGB 81 is Tiger Juden. Tiger has a set routine for checking and preparing the engine. Starting on the deck he will open the four cowl vents above the engine room. Slightly further forward and above the fuel tanks he opens the filler caps for each tank and uses the dipstick to check the fuel levels. Next he heads into the wheelhouse and to the electrical panel in the W/T office, where he switches on the boat's batteries and the engine room lights. He then turns on the fuel supply to all three diesel engines.

Next, Tiger prepares the engine room itself. The first job is to activate the engine's water-cooling system, which draws water up through the hull of the boat and into the main engine block to help cool it. After opening each of the three seacocks to the incoming pipes (one seacock per engine), Tiger checks the strainers, where the seawater passes through a fine mesh to prevent seaweed, litter or other contaminants getting into the system. Next, using the dipsticks fitted in each filler cap,

RIGHT The main power controls are found in the W/T office behind the bridge. *(Author)*

Tiger checks each engine and gearbox's oil and coolant levels.

The next step is to ensure that the Cardan shafts on each wing engine are properly greased and then to give all three engines a

BELOW One of the new water coolant system strainers fitted during the 2018 refit (see Chapter 7). The inlet pipe is fitted to the bottom of the hull and feeds water into the strainer. Its observation panel sits just above sea level, so when the glass plate is removed to clean the strainer, there is no risk of the water pressure causing it to overflow. *(PNBPT)*

BELOW RIGHT One of the three strainers as fitted. The water fills the chamber below the glass panel and passes into the outlet pipe through a fine mesh that stops contaminants such as seaweed from passing through. The seacock that opens the pipe to the sea can be seen below. There is a small amount of water visible in the bilge alongside the keel. *(Author)*

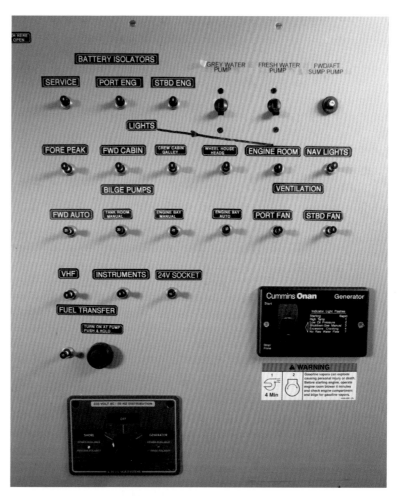

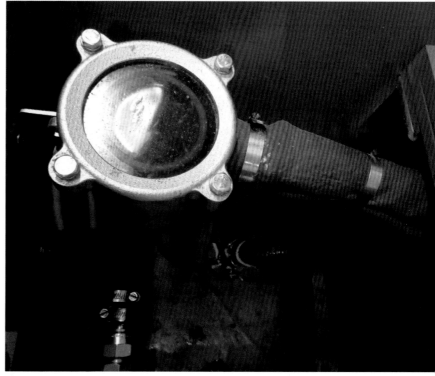

ABOVE The Cardan shaft on the port side wing engine, viewed from forward looking aft. The two wing engines' main drive outputs do not face towards the stern where the propellers are, because the engine room is too narrow to fit three engines in side by side. Instead the wing engines are positioned astern of the central engine with their drives facing forwards. The Cardan shaft provides drive to the gearbox where a vee drive system powers the main propeller shaft. *(Author)*

BELOW The port gearbox looking to port and slightly forward. The Cardan shaft runs into the gearbox and below it the main shaft runs astern to drive the propeller. The knuckle joint on the Cardan shaft next to the gearbox needs to be serviced after every 10 hours of running time. These two shafts are normally protected by a metal frame (about to be installed). The orange pipe of the seawater cooling system can be seen running from the strainer to the engine on the left. *(PNBPT)*

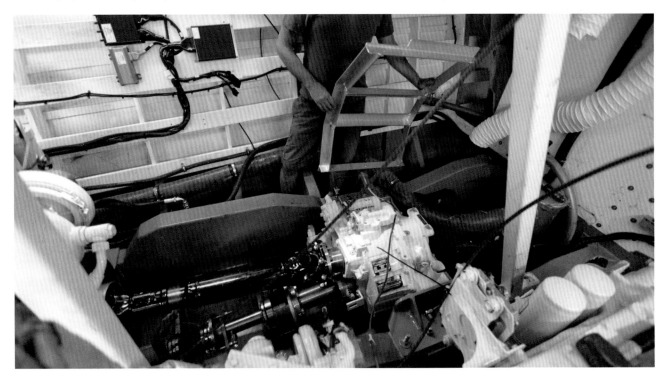

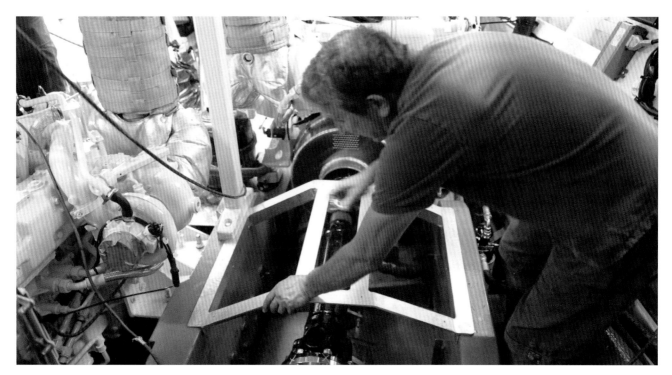

thorough visual inspection, to ensure there are no leaks, loose parts or anything else of concern. Finally, Tiger checks the water level in the bilge to ensure that there's no evidence of leaks or hull failure. It's normal to find small volumes of water in the lowest part of the boat, but significant volumes may be a sign of a more serious problem with the hull planking. Elsewhere on the boat the rest of the crew are making similar checks, ensuring there is no obvious damage to the hull.

ABOVE **The aluminium frame installed over the port wing engine shafts.** *(PNBPT)*

BELOW **The frame supports a chequer plate that covers the two shafts, which can spin up to 2,500 times per minute or more than 40 times per second.** *(PNBPT)*

Start-up

When the crew are satisfied that everything is ready and the boat is fit to put to sea, the engines will be switched on. On the bridge, Diggory inserts the keys into the three-engine ignition switches and makes a half turn on each. This activates the electrics for each engine as well as the preheaters, which begin warming the engine cylinders. A safety alarm prevents the next stage of ignition for a minimum of 10 seconds, and only once this alarm has silenced can Diggory fully ignite the engines. When he's ready, he makes the second turn of each engine key, starting with the port side engine, followed by the starboard side and finally the centre.

As the engines roar into life it's important to make sure that the exhausts are clear and that the seawater coolant is passing through cleanly. On the stern of the boat a member of the crew will observe the six exhausts (two per engine) and report back when all of them are ejecting grey smoke and water. There is not usually an equal amount passing through each, as the exhaust pipes in the engine

ABOVE The conning position on the bridge. The instrument panel was custom made by Berthon. Plastic guards cover the key ignition switches for each engine. *(Author)*

BELOW In this picture only two engines, the centre and starboard engines, have been started. There is no water coolant running out of the port-side exhausts. *(PNBPT)*

room do not equally split the water flow or exhaust gases.

With the engines running smoothly, the revs are slightly increased and then the engines are left running for 10 minutes to warm them up. Meanwhile, the crew will make the boat ready for sea, ensuring the forward 2-pounder magazine and tiller flat hatches are closed and everything in the forward accommodation spaces is secured.

The temperature gauges for each engine (the bottom left dial of each set) starts at 40°C

ABOVE MGB 81 at sea with all three engines running. It is noticeable that most of the water coolant from each engine runs out of a single exhaust with only a trickle out of the second. This is because the joints in the exhaust pipes do not split equally. *(PNBPT)*

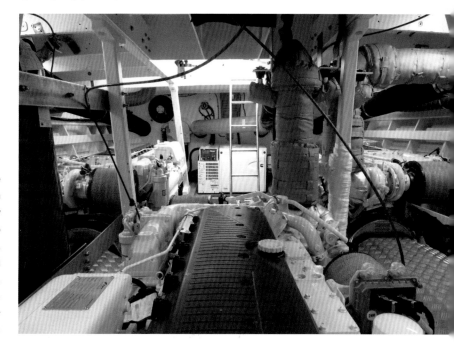

RIGHT In the engine room looking astern. The black port and starboard exhaust pipes can be seen leading astern from their respective engines. They pass through the aft bulkhead where they split into two separate exhaust outputs inside the tiller flat. The centre engine exhaust runs along the deckhead and can be seen to split behind the aft hatch ladder. The additional pipe branches away from the main path of the exhaust and consequently less water passes down it. *(Author)*

RIGHT Each of the three engines has its own gearbox, so there are three individual gear levers on the port side of the wheel on the bridge. There are only two gears for each engine, though – forward and reverse. Even when idling, the engines generate 500rpm, so as soon as the gears are put into forward – even with the throttles closed – the boat will start to move. *(Author)*

BELOW Through short switches to the different gear positions, Diggory can nurse the boat out of its berth until it is clear ahead. *(PNBPT)*

and the needles of each gauge will start to flicker when this temperature is reached, which indicates that the engines are warm enough to get under way. A final visual inspection of the gauges by Diggory, and by Tiger in the engine room, and the boat is ready to depart. Diggory gives the instruction to cast off and the boat is ready to put to sea.

Manoeuvring

Manoeuvring alongside the pontoons is done entirely using the gearboxes – switching the port and starboard engine from neutral to forward in order to turn the boat. Switching the port gearbox into forward activates the port propeller, which moves that side of the boat faster than the starboard, so the bow of the boat begins rotating to starboard. Conversely, switching the port gearbox into reverse will pull the port side backwards and the stern turns to starboard, swinging the bow to port.

Once all three engines are in forward gear, at 500rpm the engines actually generate enough power to reach 7.5kts. The speed limit inside Portsmouth Harbour itself is 10kts, so the journey from the pontoons at Boathouse 4 to the harbour entrance (a distance of approximately ¾ mile) is usually done without opening the throttles at all.

Portsmouth Harbour is a busy place. As well as Royal Navy ships regularly sailing in and out of the naval base, movements of the Isle of Wight and cross-Channel ferries, cargo ships, pleasure boats and the Portsmouth–Gosport ferry ensure that the waters are never quiet. Compared to many of these vessels, MGB 81 is considered small and is obliged to use the small boat channel on the west side of Portsmouth Harbour entrance. To cross the main channel, permission must first be received from the Queen's Harbour Master Harbour Control team, whose main office occupies the Semaphore Tower alongside Boathouse 4. From the tower and their additional offices at the harbour mouth, the harbour masters can see all vessel movements around the restricted waters and control it accordingly.

Once safely across the main channel and while the boat is heading towards the harbour entrance, the crew will monitor the engines and ensure that everything is operating smoothly. At all times it's necessary to check the engine temperatures, the rpm, the oil pressure and the alternator output. When out of the harbour mouth and at least 1,000yd from the shore, MGB 81 is free to accelerate away from the main navigation channel and into the Solent.

ABOVE However modern some of MGB 81's equipment and machinery might be, mechanically it still works much as it did in the Second World War. The gears and the throttle are not electronic; they use the same type of cable and linkage mechanism as installed by wartime boatbuilders. As a result, the gear and throttle levers do not simply slip into place – they need considerable effort to move into position. *(Author)*

ABOVE Much like the gear levers, the three throttle levers are closely spaced so that they can all be moved by one hand in a single action. With a not inconsiderable amount of effort, they are moved forward to accelerate the boat. *(Author)*

BELOW When stationary, MGB 81 is supported by buoyancy. *(PNBPT)*

RIGHT With the engines at low revolutions, MGB 81 very slowly begins to move forward. With minimal disturbance at the bow, the propellers churn the water behind the boat. *(PNBPT)*

ABOVE AND RIGHT At slow speeds she behaves much like a normal round-bilge hull. As the speed increases, the bow pushes water out of the way, generating a small bow wave. At the stern the flat bottom pushes into the water, creating a stern wake. *(PNBPT)*

LEFT As the revolutions increase and MGB 81 picks up more speed, the bow pushes water aside and up against the chine. *(PNBPT)*

LEFT As the speed increases so does the forces of the upward moving water. The chine deflects this water back down, which simultaneously creates reactionary force against the hull, pushing it upwards. *(PNBPT)*

LEFT The upward movement of the bow starts to put more weight on the stern, which pushes into the water. The wide and nearly flat bottom is similarly supported by the reactionary upward force. *(PNBPT)*

At about 1,500rpm, the engine's turbos start to engage. As speed increases, so too does the push upwards and the bow begins to lift.
(PNBPT)

ABOVE AND LEFT At the bow, the point at which it cuts through the water moves back along the keel, and the bow wave slips further down the length of the hull. *(PNBPT)*

RIGHT AND BELOW Finally, at approximately 2,000rpm and 30kts, the bow has climbed clear of the bow wave altogether and is riding on top of it. *(PNBPT)*

ABOVE AND LEFT The bow lift creates further pressure on the stern and continues to push it down, which conversely generates upward force. *(PNBPT)*

LEFT At speed, this power and the weight on the stern becomes an issue for the steering. The steering is completely mechanical with no power assistance, so as the bow lifts the rudders become heavier and it takes considerable effort to turn the wheel and direct the boat. Consequently, the turning circle widens and MGB 81 requires in excess of a quarter of a mile to make a 180-degree turn. *(PNBPT)*

BELOW In anything less than a flat-calm sea, turning would often be a wet manoeuvre. Crewmen on the stern of MGB 16 wear oilskins to protect them from the spray. *(Peter Scott)*

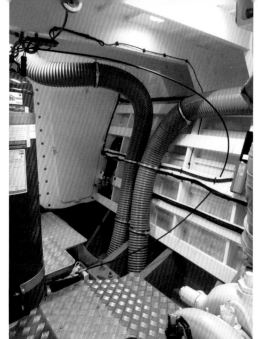

ABOVE AND ABOVE RIGHT The long blue tubes run from the cowl vents on the deck to the bilge below. *(Author)*

In the engine room

As the engines work harder, their temperatures rapidly increase. In 1942 the four cowl vents were the only ventilation to the small room – hatches were kept closed to ensure no light escaped. The cowl vents were essentially open holes to the night air – facing forwards they drew air into the engine room but could also let water splash in during rough weather. In very bad conditions the vents could be rotated to face astern.

Today there is a modern solution. The vents feed into large plastic tubes that run down to the bilge. This way, if water sprays into the cowl vents, it runs down to the bilge where it will eventually be removed by the bilge pump. The fresh air drawn in emerges from underneath the engines, further improving the ventilation. On the aft bulkhead, vents pull warm air into the tiller flat.

The seawater cooling system draws cold seawater into the engine jacket, through the oil cooler and gearbox oil coolers, into the heat

CENTRE AND LEFT On deck there is an additional form of ventilation. The ready-use ammunition lockers alongside the Oerlikon turret no longer hold ammunition – instead they hide additional vents to the engine room. In essence this is a dorade vent: air is drawn up from the gaps at the bottom of the locker and then into the vent. Water splashing across the locker cannot get into the main vent and drains off the deck instead. *(Author)*

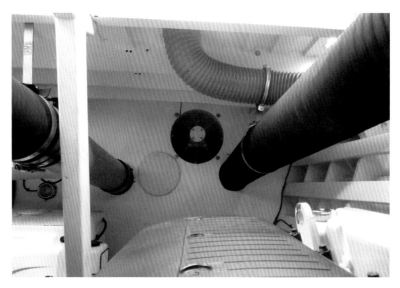

exchanger and finally into the exhaust to cool the entire exhaust system. As the boat's speed increases, more water is drawn into the system and ejects in jet streams from the exhausts. At the same time the glycol coolant is pumped around the engine block and cools boosted air through the engines' heat exchanger. Typically, the engines' temperature is approximately 85°C when they are at 2,000rpm.

Although much of MGB 81 works as it did in 1942, there are some benefits of the modern age on board. The engines are computer managed, which has several advantages. They will only allow for a maximum of 2,500rpm, which equates to approximately 34kts in average conditions. They also operate an emergency failsafe mode in the event of any malfunctions – should something go wrong with the oil pressure or alternator output, the computer shuts the engines down to a 'limp' mode that prevents them from suffering any further damage, while allowing just enough power for the boat to sail home. On the bridge Diggory has the benefit of a multi-display unit, which is usually programmed to display the depth of water and the boat's speed over ground.

Shutdown

Returning to Portsmouth Harbour, the engine revolutions are lowered to 500rpm so that the speed limit can be adhered to. This gives the engines time to cool and they have usually reached 40–50°C before MGB 81 reaches its berth. Manoeuvring is once again conducted using the gears. The engine room fans will normally be left running for some time to properly vent the exhausts from the enclosed space. When she's fully shut down, MGB 81's covers are put over the bridge, the forward gun and the Lewis guns until she's next ready to put to sea.

BELOW MGB 81 tied up behind Boathouse 4 in Portsmouth Historic Dockyard. *(PNBPT)*

Chapter Six

MGB 81's story

MGB 81's service in the Second World War, and the numerous actions she participated in, are indicative of the story of all Coastal Forces vessels. At the same time, MGB 81's story would be special even if she did not survive today.

OPPOSITE MTB 416 (ex-MGB 81) leads boats of the 1st MTB Flotilla after a patrol off the Normandy coast in June 1944. *(CFHT Collection)*

The birth of MGB 81

MGB 81 was originally part of an order for three MA/SB flotillas placed on 27 November 1940. When the designs for the new Mk V MGB were accepted by the Admiralty in February 1941, the order was updated – the 24 boats were to be completed as MGBs 74–97 (this order was reduced to a single flotilla, pennants 74–81, in March 1941, although the remaining two flotillas were eventually reinstated). As the final boat in the order, MGB 81, yard number 1807, was the last to be started: her keel was laid down on 16 December 1941, a full year after design work on the Mk V had commenced.

By July 1942, MGBs 74–78 had arrived at HMS *Beehive* – the Coastal Forces base at Felixstowe where Hichens' 6th MGB Flotilla were based – and were working alongside the 70ft boats of the 6th MGB Flotilla. At the same time,

Sub Lieutenant J.A. Cowley left *Beehive* and travelled to Hythe to stand by MGB 81. Cowley had previously been in command of MGB 58 (originally ordered as a French MTB and briefly commissioned as an MA/SB before conversion to an MGB) but had only seen action while first lieutenant on MGB 61. Cowley was from the Isle of Man and was known to almost everyone as Kelly, a common Manx name, and was the most junior CO in Hichens' MGB flotilla. Hichens himself described him thus:

Small and slight with a large nose, generally referred to as the 'Dreaded Beak', and a fearsome pipe, the smell from which was calculated to turn all stomachs but its owner's, he was always being twitted for being behind station and losing contact. This was quite unjustified, but it clung to him and in later days a boat returning one evening met a unit of the flotilla going to sea and made the classic remark that 'he had met the flotilla and Kelly'. [1]

At British Power Boat, Cowley was joined by his new first lieutenant, Sub Lieutenant Richard Crosley, and the crew of ratings. There is no record of the circumstances of 81's launch on 26 June 1942, but many boats first entered the water with little or no ceremony in the busy boat yard. She underwent her Admiralty acceptance trials on 8 July and on the successful conclusion of the test (where she reached 38kts), the boat was officially accepted into the Royal Navy. Three days later, on 11 July, MGB 81 was formally commissioned: the British Power Boat pennant was hauled down and the White Ensign was raised up the mast. Her next destination was the working-up base HMS *Bee* at Weymouth.

While Cowley was away, Hichens' swollen command finally divided into two separate units when, in response to the attack on convoy WP 183, the 8th MGB Flotilla was formed and abruptly sent to Cornwall. When MGB 81 was fully worked up, she sailed to Dartmouth to join her sister boats on 1 August. For the first time the 8th MGB Flotilla was a complete eight-boat unit.

BELOW MTB 459 during her working-up at HMS *Bee*, Holyhead, in early 1944. *(Library and Archives Canada/ PA-144589)*

1   Hichens, 1944, pp. 72–73.

ROBERT HICHENS

Robert Peverell Hichens was born in March 1909 and pursued a career in law before the Second World War. He also enjoyed sailing for sport and pleasure and in the 1930s joined the Royal Navy Volunteer Supplementary Reserve, an additional branch of the established RNVR that provided the Admiralty with a core of capable sailors.

When war broke out Hichens was called up in October 1939 and commissioned as a sub lieutenant. He joined the minesweeper HMS *Halcyon* as a lieutenant in December before moving to HMS *Niger*, which he was with during the Dunkirk evacuation in the summer. During the evacuation, Hichens took charge of a number of small boats and in doing so was able to help rescue several hundred men, for which he was awarded the Distinguished Service Cross (DSC).

For some time Hichens had been interested in Coastal Forces and in October 1940, he was appointed to HMS *Osprey* at Portland. The following month he was given his first seagoing command: MA/SB 16. Within two weeks he'd been moved to MA/SB 18 and then MA/SB 14 in December. The constant moves were a result of the Admiralty's rapid rearming of the MA/SBs, but 14 was destined for training duties at HMS *St Christopher* in Fort William, Scotland, and Hichens made the journey up the west coast in two days. Only a few weeks later he was back on the south coast, standing by MGB 64 at British Power Boat. On 11 February 1941, he commissioned the latest gun boat to enter service with the Royal Navy.

Hichens and his crew joined the 6th MGB Flotilla, forming at Fowey in Cornwall. His was the only boat under the command of an RNVR officer but it did not take long for him to win the respect of the other boats' skippers. When the senior officer departed in August, Hichens was promoted to lieutenant commander and took over, becoming the first RNVR officer to command a flotilla.

Hichens was determined that his flotilla should find the best way to engage the S-boats, their principal opponents. He trained his crews to deal with any possible contingency at sea so that when action did come, everyone would know instinctively what was required of them. Despite the long months with no sight of an

ABOVE Robert Hichens, back row third from left, with his crew on MGB 78. *(Author's Collection)*

enemy vessel, his perseverance paid off when MGBs 64 and 67 surprised five S-boats on the night of 19 November 1941, earning him a bar to his DSC. The action the following April, in which he engaged a flotilla of S-boats outside Ostend Harbour, earned him a Distinguished Service Order (DSO).

When he took command of the new Mk V boats and formed the 8th MGB Flotilla, Hichens was finally able to compete on better terms with the S-boats. Success was not long in coming and actions were fought around Normandy and the Channel Islands, earning a bar to his DSO after the July 1942 action against an enemy trawler off Alderney. A second bar to the DSC was awarded for the action off the Hook of Holland on the night of 14 September that year.

Hichens declined a shore role and fought hard to get his flotilla's potential recognised, lobbying the Admiralty to fit torpedoes to their boats. Before his entreaties bore fruit, he was killed on the night of 12/13 April 1943 while engaging enemy flak trawlers. His loss sent shockwaves through Coastal Forces, who fully recognised his role in establishing the best principles and tactics for using MGBs.

With two Distinguished Service Orders, three Distinguished Service Crosses and three Mentions in Despatches, he remains the most decorated officer in the history of the RNVR. In 1942 he began writing his wartime memoirs, *We Fought Them in Gunboats*, which were published posthumously in 1944.

RIGHT The Royal Dart Hotel at Kingswear was the headquarters of HMS *Cicala*, the Coastal Forces base on the Dart.
(Geoff Sheppard)

Early operations

On the night of 1 August, Hichens led four boats of his flotilla on the offensive patrol that achieved such success outside the breakwater at Cherbourg. MGB 81 was not among them but she would not have long to wait for her first active patrol. Two nights later, at 10:30pm on 3 August 1942, MGB 81 set sail with MGBs 74, 75 and 76 on her first operation. Hichens sailed with Lieutenant

Commander Robert Campbell on MGB 76 (his usual boat MGB 77 was still undergoing repairs at Poole). Lieutenant Tommy Ladner followed on MGB 75 and Lieutenant Rodney Sykes on MGB 74. As the new boat, Cowley brought up the rear on MGB 81.

That night Convoy PW 196 sailed from Portsmouth, bound for Milford Haven. Operation NH-1, the defence of the merchant ships against S-boat attacks, saw two destroyers patrolling south of the Needles and three MTBs patrolling north of the Bay of Seine. Hichens' MGBs were ordered to proceed south-east from Dartmouth to an initial patrol line running from approximately 20 miles due north to approximately 20 miles north-west of Guernsey. There they'd await information on enemy vessels and engage them accordingly. The destroyers and MTBs were to keep to the east side of Cherbourg and the MGBs to the west, unless the Commander-in-Chief of Portsmouth Command allowed otherwise. MGBs blundering unannounced into the destroyers' zone were likely to attract all the wrong sort of attention.

Eric Archer, who later commanded 81, recalled the typical start of a patrol:

Proceeding to sea on operations from Dartmouth, once clear of the entrance, guns would be tested on the Mewstone, a large rock to starboard which sparked with explosive bursts from our 2-pounder pom-pom, Oerlikon and Vickers guns. ...

BELOW The Mew Stone off Dartmouth, a regular target for MGB 81's gun.
(Derek Harper)

We usually cruised in quarter-line formation to port of the senior officer to facilitate station keeping as each coxswain was on the starboard side of the bridge. To maintain close station, one steered just clear of the wake of the next ahead and just astern of the plume.[2]

Once on station, Hichens usually slowed his boats down or stopped to save fuel and reduce noise. From their position that night, they'll have been able to see the lighthouses of Alderney and Guernsey – assuming that they were lit as they had been on previous nights. The sea would lap against the hulls of the boats or, if it was a little rougher, thud against the planking, rolling the boats this way and that. The crews will doubtless have been itching to manoeuvre closer to Cherbourg to repeat the success of two nights before, or Alderney to repeat the attack of two weeks previously. But with a convoy to protect this time, there could be no distractions. Instead the MGBs waited. And waited.

Hichens' boats saw no action that night. Their orders required them to be heading well away from the French coast by first light and doubtless, when they returned to Dartmouth on the morning of 5 August, they will have been disgusted to hear that the S-boats had slipped past them.

Convoy PW 196 came under air attack at around the same time that the MGBs left Dartmouth. Six torpedo-carrying Heinkel He 111s approached from the east and, despite the best efforts of escort destroyers HMS *Blencathra* and *Tynedale*, a tanker was damaged by a torpedo. *Tynedale* remained with the tanker while *Blencathra* continued with the convoy and while south of Devon at about 1:15am, she sighted at least four S-boats. For the next three hours, *Blencathra* fought a running battle with the torpedo boats, placing herself between them and the convoy and using starshell to illuminate the sea and fire on the little boats. At least five torpedo tracks were seen, but *Blencathra*'s actions prevented any further casualties.

In fact, 19 S-boats had sailed that night,

although only 16 reached the area to launch their 'stab' attack on the convoy. The crews claimed that two merchant ships were sunk and a third damaged, although even this would have been a poor result for the number of boats involved in the attack – the fact that none were hit by the S-boats would have galled them further. In any case it was almost the end of the stab attack in the Channel that year – PW 197's sailing was delayed in light of the events of that night and the Royal Navy quickly altered their sailing schedule to ensure that no convoys were between Land's End and Portsmouth after dark.

MGB 81's first operation will have been a disappointment for her crew, but it wasn't an unusual night. Coastal Forces' actions were typified by long periods of waiting, sometimes with no activity for weeks at a time. Thus, at 10:30pm on 5 August, 81 set out with Hichens in MGB 80 and accompanied by 74 and 78, this time with the objective of destroying S-boats around Guernsey. Free of the need to protect a convoy, this was a hunting patrol at Hichens' discretion, but even he couldn't magic S-boats out of thin air and the patrol returned empty handed at 6:40 the next morning.

That lunchtime, Cowley entertained Hichens and the other officers with gin in 81's wardroom. Suddenly a message was delivered for Hichens to take a telephone call and he clambered, wearily, on to the deck of their depot ship HMS *Aberdonian*. Moments later he ran back into the wardroom to rouse the officers of 75, 78 and 81 and within five more minutes the three boats were powering out of Dartmouth Harbour. An aircraft had come down only 30 miles north of the Brittany coast.

Speeding south with an escort of Spitfires overhead, the boats split up and searched the target area approximately 4 miles apart. Suddenly MGB 75 sped off and then came to a stop. A Czech airman was pulled aboard who related, in broken English, that there may have been another pilot somewhere to the east. Hichens conducted another search but with no one to be seen, and with the fighter escort having turned for home owing to a lack of fuel, they returned to Dartmouth, miraculously unmolested by German aircraft.

---

2   Selman, p. 9.

While naval ratings were entitled to a daily tot of rum, spirits tended to be more popular among the officers. In late 1942, Hichens observed on entering 81's wardroom that

on the locker tops was assembled the most astonishing selection of bottles. Six bottles of gin, six of rum, six of whisky, and lo and behold! even six of brandy! It made you feel cheerful just to see the rows of bottles, and Kelly was much commended on his zeal and general spirit of social welfare by all and sundry.[3]

It was in the wardroom of MGB 81 on 6 August 1942 that 'Kelly' Cowley created the Mark VIII. In his book, *We Fought Them in Gunboats*, Hichens recalled its origins.

It was mid-day, gin time, and Kelly had just performed prodigies with the bottles. We were all dead tired. I had slumped into a half recumbent posture on the wardroom settee and shut my eyes:

'What will you have, sir?'

'Oh, anything and everything, Kelly,' I replied without looking up.

Kelly took me at my word. He picked up a gin bottle in one hand, a rum bottle in the other, and poured in a liberal dose simultaneously. Then he picked up the lemon squash and orange squash and applied them also together, finishing off with water.

Thus was born the flotilla's famous Mark VIII. I can recommend it as a delicious drink and a remarkable reviver.[4]

Later that year the drink was enhanced by Cowley and Crosely with the addition of a dash of brandy to create the Mark VIII C, 'a definitely sound and progressive modification'.

BELOW The wardroom of MGB 16. *(Peter Scott)*

3   Hichens, 1944, p. 147.

4   Hichens, 1944, p. 127.

Action at last

Poor weather disrupted the next patrol planned for the night of the 11th. The same operation was scheduled for the 13th and, at 9:30pm, MGBs 77, 78, 80 and 81 sailed from Dartmouth to conduct a patrol along a line from approximately 15 miles west to 15 miles north of Guernsey. Hichens' orders specified that he was free to seek out targets beyond this line if nothing had been seen by 2:00am, but he apparently made up his mind 90 minutes early, reporting that it was certain that any S-boats bound for the coast would have passed them by then. Instead he led the boats to a position 2 miles south of St Martin's Point, the promontory at the south-east corner of Guernsey.

At 2:10am an echo was picked up on the RDF just over half a mile away. The MGBs slowly and silently crept up towards the target on their auxiliary engines and four minutes later a pair of large trawlers were spotted ahead, one on each beam. Manoeuvring carefully, the four boats came up close alongside the starboard boat until, when they were at point-blank range, a German sentry finally noticed them and flashed a challenge with a signal light.

Immediately all four MGBs opened fire. The combined firepower of four 2-pounders, eight Oerlikons and as many Lewis guns as could be brought to bear hammered into the trawler. Surprised and immediately supressed by the MGBs' weight of arms, the trawler barely managed to make any return fire as the MGBs circled around her, riddling the enemy vessel with gunfire.

The second trawler now opened fire with what were judged by the British crews to be a 4in gun, 2-pounders and 20mm. Hichens led his line of boats to circle the new target at approximately 200m range. Heavy fire poured into the trawler but suddenly an unseen third enemy vessel began to fire on the MGBs. Deciding not to chance their luck any further, Hichens ordered the MGBs to disengage and head for home, and not a moment too soon.

BELOW A German armed trawler, or *Vorpostenboot*. Although slow, these boats were well armed and had good sea-keeping qualities. *(Municipal Archives of Trondheim, Norway)*

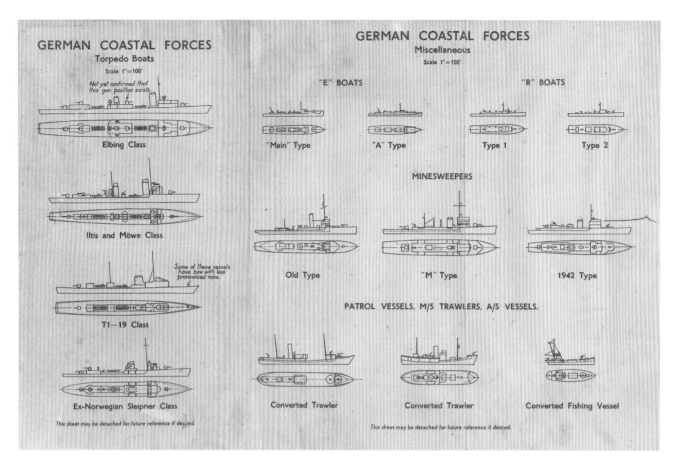

GERMAN COASTAL FORCES
Torpedo Boats
Scale 1"=100'

Not yet confirmed that this gun position exists

Elbing Class

Iltis and Möwe Class

Some of these vessels have bow with less pronounced rake.

T1—19 Class

Ex-Norwegian Sleipner Class

This sheet may be detached for future reference if desired.

GERMAN COASTAL FORCES
Miscellaneous
Scale 1"=100'

"E" BOATS

"Main" Type

"A" Type

"R" BOATS

Type 1

Type 2

MINESWEEPERS

Old Type

"M" Type

1942 Type

PATROL VESSELS, M/S TRAWLERS, A/S VESSELS.

Converted Trawler

Converted Trawler

Converted Fishing Vessel

This sheet may be detached for future reference if desired.

ABOVE A Coastal Forces ID chart, issued to help crews recognise enemy vessels. *(Diggory Rose Collection)*

As they pulled away, Lieutenant Ronald Carr on the bridge of MGB 80 was struck through the chest by a bullet. The crew signalled Hichens who led them back as fast as the Packards would allow, but at the back of the line, Cowley lived up to his reputation and became separated. Straining through the darkness, the crew of MGB 81 were unable to see any of their fellow charges and, with fire continuing to stream into the night sky behind them, Cowley steered 81 back independently.

Hichens' haste was rewarded when Carr was whisked to a hospital and operated on, bringing him back from the verge of certain death. In fact, Carr had been unlucky – most of the damage to the MGBs had been superficial. On the other hand, the crews had left the Channel Islands hopeful that one of the trawlers was in sinking condition, especially as German sailors had even been seen scrambling to abandon ship. In fact, no German losses were reported that night around the Channel Islands, so the vessel was probably salvaged, but it was a successful first encounter with the enemy for MGB 81 and a clear victory for the British.

The action was MGB 81's last patrol into the Channel that year. A few nights later three boats of the flotilla went out, but without incident. On the night of the 18th, two offensive patrols sailed, each consisting of three MGBs and one or two MTBs of the 21st MTB Flotilla. Again, no enemy vessels were encountered, likely a result in Hichens opinion, of the din made by the older Vosper boats. Another patrol two nights later similarly yielded no contact.

In fact, by mid-August only one flotilla of S-boats remained at Cherbourg, while the 2nd and 4th had returned to the North Sea. Accordingly, on 21 August the 8th MGB Flotilla received instruction to return to Felixstowe, where they arrived on the 24th.

Over to the east coast

Now MGB 81 would settle into the routine that had characterised the careers of the 70ft whalebacks. On the night of 26 August, no fewer than 17 MGBs patrolled the North Sea, including MGB 81 and four more Mk Vs from the 8th MGB Flotilla, five Elcos from the

7th Flotilla, four whalebacks from the 5th and 6th Flotillas and three Fairmile Cs from the 12th and 16th MGB Flotillas. Frustratingly, the gremlins that had haunted Hichens previously returned, with five boats breaking down, including three of the Mk Vs. No contact was made that night, nor when 81 next went out to patrol off the Hook of Holland with MGBs 76, 78 and 79 five nights later.

September initially began much the same way. MGB 81's first operation that month was to join five more MGBs escorting four Fairmile As of the 51st ML Flotilla on a minelaying operation off the Hook of Holland on the night of the 7th. This was cancelled owing to the weather and 81 instead spent her first night on the Z line. However, the minelaying operation eventually went ahead on the night of the 10th with MGBs 75, 76, 77 and 81 supporting MLs 105, 106 and 110.

Hichens took his group to stand off a few miles north-east of the intended minefield. As the MLs began their first run to lay their deadly cargo, two enemy trawlers suddenly appeared through the gloom and immediately opened fire. Although ML 106 managed to lay six mines before retiring, the rest were jettisoned to hasten the Fairmiles' escape.

Hearing the gunfire in the distance, the MGBs roared towards the action. The MLs were spotted scurrying westward, but before the crews had a chance to search for the trawlers, the sea around them suddenly erupted with great geysers of spray. To the east one of the coastal batteries of the Atlantic Wall had been alerted to the Royal Navy's presence and using their radar-guided guns began to fire on the small boats. A splinter tore into MGB 81's hull, fortunately inflicting only light damage, before Cowley steered her away from danger.

Although the minelaying mission was over, the MGBs remained off the Dutch coast for some time hoping to surprise S-boats returning from the coast of East Anglia. Instead it was the Fairmile Cs of the 16th MGB Flotilla that intercepted a group of returning S-boats, engaging them in the vicinity of the Brown Bank (in the middle of the North Sea, east of Great Yarmouth). A fierce engagement followed, and Hichens' MGBs rushed to assist but without making contact. The capture of

ABOVE **A fuel tank is hoisted from the hull of a 70ft MGB during a service at HMS *Beehive*.** *(IWM A18709)*

BELOW **Coastal Forces crews collect thermos flasks and sandwiches in advance of a night patrol from HMS *Beehive* in November 1942. Note the oilskin jacket.** *(IWM A12912)*

ABOVE Able Seaman J.C. Egginton carries out the traditional 'dhobying' – washing his clothes in front of a 2-pounder. Behind him is a one-piece waterproof quilted suit, which started to become standard issue in 1942. *(IWM A22912)*

MGBs 77, 81, 75', which rather suggests only cosmetic damage. It's interesting to compare this with Hichens' own account, given in *We Fought Them in Gunboats*:

> *My boat had been hit several times, and I fancied some had been in the engine room. I sent for Stay [Petty Officer Motor Mechanic Vic Stay]. A face appeared, covered in blood and oil, unrecognisable until the familiar words came: 'Top line sir. One of the oil tanks is stuffed up with a rag and I had to plug one of the exhaust pipe jackets. But she'll be all right.'*
>
> *Some motor mechanics could be worth their weight in gold. A shell had exploded in the engine room, slightly wounding Stay in the face, puncturing one of the oil tanks and putting a hole in the exhaust pipe jacket. With jets of intensely hot oil and sea water pouring over him, Stay had promptly plugged both holes and kept the engine running without a falter.[5]*

MGB 335 that night would further hinder 81's operations in the future, as the charts found by the Germans indicated numerous interception spots that the S-boats subsequently avoided.

On the night of 14 September, the MLs returned to the Hook of Holland to complete their mission. Once again Hichens led the covering force in MGB 77, accompanied by 75, 76 and 81. This time the minelaying passed without incident and as the MLs turned west for home, the gun boats headed closer to the enemy coast.

At 3:20am the boats' hydrophones picked up a distant murmur. Stealing closer to the coast the MGBs sighted a small convoy making for the Hook and the canal into Rotterdam. They were in fact so close to the canal that the two merchant vessels, estimated to be approximately 500 and 700 tons, had pulled ahead of their escorts, meaning that the four MGBs had a few minutes' uninterrupted firing on the ships. A little later, four armed trawlers finally caught up and a tougher battle ensued. Hits were scored on all four trawlers, but their own gunfire caused damage on the gun boats in return. The Admiralty War Diary records that there was 'superficial damage to

The severity of damage caused to 81 isn't recorded, but it was not enough to be noted on the ship's record card. Nonetheless, it wasn't until the night of 25 September that any of the 8th Flotilla were back on patrol again, when MGBs 76, 78 and 81 spent a night on the Z line, waiting at Z 11 for an enemy that never appeared. Nor was there any change the following night when they were joined by 77. Four nights later the four boats headed further into the North Sea on patrol, again without success. But if the crews were yearning action, they didn't have long to wait.

The reality of war

Until now, Hichens' crews had led fairly charmed lives, with little loss relative to the damage they had meted out to the enemy. That would change in October.

On the night of 2/3 October, Hichens, in MGB 77, led 78, 81 and 60 (one of the whalebacks of the 6th Flotilla) to patrol off the Hook of Holland. On this occasion, Cowley wasn't aboard – it wasn't unusual for boats

---

5   Hichens, 1944, pp. 136–37.

LEFT MTBs 447 and 449, ex-MGBs 128 and 130 respectively. *(CFHT Collection)*

BELOW S 204, a 100-class S-boat after its surrender at the end of the war. In 1942 the Kriegsmarine introduced the 'skull cap' armoured dome over the S-boats' bridge in response to the heavier armament of the MGBs.
(CFHT Collection)

to periodically swap skippers if one was on leave or on a training course, and tonight 81 was commanded by Sub Lieutenant Rodney Sykes. At 1:34am four enemy trawlers were spotted approximately 10 miles from the Dutch coast and, after a little manoeuvring, the boats were ready to launch an attack. MGBs 77, 81 and 60 crept around to the stern of the line of enemy ships that were heading south-west, while Lieutenant George Duncan on 78 raced ahead in order to make a depth-charge attack across their bows.

At 1:50am the three MGBs astern closed and attacked the trawlers, creating a distraction for Duncan before he roared in with his depth charges. Five minutes later, tracer fire was seen in the south-west, indicating 78 was making its attack. At 2:10am Hichens and his boats disengaged and slipped away to a rendezvous to the east as a fog came down across the area. Shortly afterwards, the crews of the three boats saw tracer being fired into the air, an agreed signal of distress in the flotilla. A search followed and efforts were made to contact 78 by wireless, but the boat was nowhere to be found. Hichens headed north in response to a request from some nearby MTBs, but when they returned to Felixstowe, 78 had not appeared.

MGBs 75, 76 and 81, accompanied by boats of the 6th Flotilla, set out before darkness fell on the 3rd to search for 78 but without success. It wasn't until sometime later that the facts became clear – Duncan had been killed on the run-in and although the crew completed the depth-charge attack, the boat was badly damaged on striking a sandbank and the crew were forced to abandon ship. The loss cast a pall over the flotilla, made worse when MGB 76 was also lost three nights later.

The rest of the month was quiet for the flotilla, with only a few patrols and 81 herself only taking part in a sweep off the Hook of Holland on the night of 30 October that yielded no results. She made patrols and provided further escort duty for minelaying MLs on 1, 4, 9, 11 and 14 November, followed by more of the same on 3, 12 and 19 December. In the New Year it wasn't until 18 January that 81 was out on patrol again, then on the 22nd and 24th when the only incident of note was a

collision between MGBs 74 and 80. In fact no boats of the flotilla saw any hint of the enemy over this period.

The enforced respite allowed the flotilla to reconsolidate. MGB 111, under Lieutenant John Mathias, and 112, under Lieutenant Derek Sidebottom, arrived to replace 78 and 76 respectively. The flotilla was swelled by the arrival of MGB 115 in January 1943, commanded by the now fully recovered Ronald Carr with Sub Lieutenant Eric Archer as his first lieutenant. Robert Campbell took command of MGB 75, with a young Sub Lieutenant Charles Cameron Gough as his first lieutenant.

The flotilla also began experimenting with their armament. The Holman Projector on the stern was a pointless addition to their firepower and AA defence was rarely required anyway, given that most of their operations were at night. Hichens was convinced that the power-operated twin Oerlikon turret was unnecessarily complicated and that a hand-trained version, lighter and less prone to defects, could be equally effective. Lieutenant Woods' prototype twin gun mount had been installed on MGB 79 but by the New Year several more boats, including 81, were sporting an additional Oerlikon or two on their sterns.

More losses

February began much like the previous months with the flotilla spending undisturbed nights on the Z line. MGB 81 herself patrolled Z 12 on the 4th and Z 51 on the 19th. The following night, MGBs 74, 77 and 112 set off to patrol off IJmuiden on the Dutch coast when defects forced 74 to return to base. Cowley scrambled his crew and 81 sailed, rushing to catch up with his colleagues. Once the force was together they moved close to the coast when suddenly they were fired on by two M-class minesweepers. It was another example of the sort of target that a torpedo-equipped MGB might have been able to tackle, but their guns alone would not be able to compete with the minesweepers. Deciding that discretion was the better part of valour, they withdrew without returning fire, but it would not be long before they had another chance to use their guns.

ABOVE

A *Vorpostenboot*, one of the heavily armed and strengthened trawlers. *(Bundesarchiv)*

On the night of 24/25 February, 81 had another quiet night on the Z line, but three nights later she sailed with Hichens on 77, Lieutenant David James on 79 and Mathias on 111. Joining them were MTBs 70, 32, 69 and 72 of the 4th MTB Flotilla and Fairmile As 106, 100 and 110 of the 51st ML Flotilla, for a mixed operation off the Dutch coast.

The MLs laid their mines and at 1:00am on the 28th sailed west for home. Their escort work completed, Hichens led the MGBs to a position north of The Hague where they picked up a convoy with their RDF and hydrophones. Closing, they found a large 5,000-ton merchant vessel accompanied by armed trawlers and minesweepers. A signal was sent to the MTBs, but they were having their own problems, having accidentally entered a German minefield, and were not instantly on hand to assist. Instead Hichens shadowed the convoy, but the boats were spotted and came under heavy fire. Hichens led them south, hoping to work between the convoy and the Hook of Holland.

At 3:11am a red light was spotted to seawards, suggesting that the boats had indeed got between the harbour and the convoy. As Hichens prepared to position his boats to attack

the merchant vessel, at 3:20am an escort minesweeper hove into view and a sharp gun battle ensued for the next five minutes.

By the time the boats withdrew to the south-west, they believed they'd made significant hits on a number of escort vessels, but it quickly became apparent that 79 was no longer with them. In fact James had sighted another target, but as he moved to engage, heavy gunfire slammed into the boat. The fuel tanks exploded, power was lost and the boat quickly became ablaze. As James himself manned the only operational heavy gun position – the hand-trained twin Oerlikon mount on the stern – the Lewis gunners fired tracer into the air.

Seeing the distress signal, Hichens led his three boats back to the east and immediately sighted the blazing MGB 79, with the crew approximately 40m away clinging to a life raft. Cowley circled around releasing acrid chemical smoke from the smoke pot on the stern in an effort to shield Hichens and Mathias, who went in to try to take the crew aboard. Instead a stiff breeze quickly dispersed the smoke and the enemy closed on the mercy mission, inflicting heavy fire into all three boats; 77 and 111 managed to rescue seven men before they were compelled to withdraw, although two were then killed as gunfire crashed through the boats. MGB 77 raced away with smoke billowing from a fire in the wireless room which was only eventually extinguished by smashing a hole into the wheelhouse roof and pouring seawater in.

As the MGBs disengaged, the MTBs finally caught up and made their attack on the convoy, but without success. Eventually they were able to rendezvous with the MGBs and the wounded party sailed for home.

All three gunboats sustained damage and took eight casualties of their own, in addition to those from 79. Four men, including James, had to be left in the water, although they were picked up by the Germans and became prisoners of war. MGB 81 was hit four times, one of which struck the engine room and knocked out power to the Oerlikon turret.

On 7/8 March, 81 was back out with 80 and 111 escorting the MLs of the 51st Flotilla, while 11/12 March found her on the Z line once again. The following night she sailed on another combined MGB, MTB and minelaying ML operation off the Dutch coast, although the mine lay was scrubbed due to the weather and the boats all returned unmolested the following morning. When 81 next put to sea again on the 17th, the minelaying was successful, although the MTBs and MGBs again failed to make any contact with enemy vessels. On the nights of 21/22 and 27/28 March, she returned to the Z line, silently watching for S-boats that never came. For the first time on the latter night, 81 served as the senior officer's boat. It's possible that Hichens himself was aboard, or equally possible that Cowley was in charge of the three boats of the group. In the very early hours of the 29th, 81 again acted as the senior boat when she, 111 and 112 put to sea at 3:36am. This may have been to support some Fairmile C MGBs that had encountered S-boats on the Z line, but the action was well over by the time the British Power Boats arrived and they returned to harbour six hours later. March ended as quietly as it had started for the 8th Flotilla.

April began, as it so often does in Britain, with rough weather. All Coastal Forces operations on the east coast were cancelled on the 1st, and then on the 5th for three nights running owing to storms. As the weather slowly cleared, boats of the 8th Flotilla returned to the Z line and eventually to the Dutch coast, where, in the early hours of the 13th, Hichens was killed. His death sent shockwaves through Coastal Forces, but especially his own flotilla.

The month ended with the weather scrubbing operations once again. The operations log doesn't record MGB 81 sailing at all in April, but on the 29th she began a refit at Brightlingsea, the main Coastal Forces repair base for vessels on the east coast. It's possible that as well as the weather, defects had blighted 81 that month, eventually forcing her to visit a dedicated repair yard. On the same day that 81 sailed to Brightlingsea, MGBs 75, 80, 111 and 115 of the much-diminished 8th MGB Flotilla sailed for Dartmouth.

Back in the Channel

The flotilla began to rebuild itself on the south coast. John Mathias had temporarily commanded after Hichens' death, but Lieutenant F.N. Stephenson formally became senior officer in Dartmouth.

MGB 81's repairs were completed on 20 May and she sailed round the coast to Dartmouth to rejoin the flotilla. Unfortunately, it was not a long stay – on 6 June, 81 and 115 collided, resulting in damage to the hull below the waterline for Cowley's newly repaired command. On the 14th she was taken into the British Power Boat yard in Poole Harbour for further repairs and remained there until 23 July.

On her return to the water, MGB 81 was given a new crew when that of MGB 80 transferred to her. The new skipper was a New Zealander, Lieutenant John Mallitte, who had previously commanded 74 at Felixstowe before taking command of 80 in August 1942. His first lieutenant was Sub Lieutenant Derek Okey who, as a midshipman, had been wounded on the bridge of MGB 112 when Hichens was killed. They were joined by a third officer, Sub Lieutenant Robin Coventry.

Increased S-boat activity had brought the flotilla back to the Channel again, but by August only the 4th and 5th S-boat Flotillas remained in Cherbourg and by September even the 4th had returned to the North Sea. The MGBs spent their time patrolling near the French coast, often accompanied by MTBs of the 23rd MTB Flotilla, a unit crewed entirely by Free Frenchmen. At least once, 81 patrolled off the Eddystone Rocks in the Channel, but her only two actions in this period came on the nights of 10/11 and 11/12 September, the former when she patrolled off the Channel Islands, accompanied by 111 and MTBs 94 and 90.

In the early hours of the 11th, the boats saw a succession of Very lights in the distance and, on closing, spotted four small boats near Guernsey. Closer investigation revealed two armed trawlers leading a *schuyt* (a flat-bottomed sailing barge) and a small trawler in a column approximately half a mile long. The MGBs stealthily crept up to make an attack and distract the vessels long enough for the MTBs to close the distance and launch a torpedo attack.

MGB 111 led 81 in a charge towards the head of the column, engaging each ship in turn as they passed down their port side at a range of 400m. The enemy returned fire ineffectually and the MGBs were able to concentrate their fire on the last boat in line, causing a number of explosions aboard. Meanwhile, the MTBs came in from the starboard side – 94 fired

two torpedoes at the leading trawler followed by 90 who fired one, although apparently without success. Five minutes after the action had started the boats pulled away, 111 with a jammed 40mm pom-pom.

Although the MTBs had expended three of their four torpedoes, the MGBs didn't receive

a signal to indicate the attack was over and so continued to shadow the convoy towards Jersey. At 2:56am the two boats roared into attack again before the column reached the shelter of the coast; 111 had not been able to clear her pom-pom and, two minutes later, 81's jammed as well. As the enemy's fire was becoming more accurate, the boats now sensibly withdrew. Both boats claimed numerous hits on the column when they returned to Dartmouth and had avoided any serious damage or casualties themselves.

The following evening 81 set out again on a sweep for further enemy shipping with MGBs 80, 75 and 111. This time their journey took them to the north-west side of the Cherbourg Peninsula and at 2:32am on the 12th, lights were switched on at Alderney and Cap de la Hague, which suggested a convoy might be imminent. Instead, a coastal battery suddenly boomed out and large splashes some 25m high exploded around the boats. The crews observed that the fire seemed to come in four-gun salvoes from slightly west of Cap de la Hague. It's possible that this was actually Battery StP 356 Auderville-Laye, equipped with a pair of 15cm guns and two 20cm railway guns, which would certainly explain the tall plumes of water. The first two salvoes were uncomfortably accurate (landing within 10m of the boats) and the MGBs hastily beat a retreat, pursued by four more salvoes. A direct hit would most certainly have destroyed a boat and killed everyone on it.

MGB 81 suffered some minor damage in these encounters and on the 16th she found herself at British Power Boat's yard in Poole once again. As well as repairs to the damaged hull, she received new rudders during her stay.

A new identity

The biggest change that would occur in the summer of 1943 was the redesignation of all 'short' MGBs. Hichens had long lobbied for torpedo tubes on his boats and finally the Admiralty had seen sense. After the experiments with MGBs 77 and 123, the decision was made that all new boats would be completed as MTBs and that the existing core of Mk V British Power Boats would be redesignated MTBs. An official order dated to 23 August specified the change of identity, although the authority to make this conversion was left to local commands. Plymouth Command apparently did not confirm 81's change until she was at Poole in September.

Thus MGB 81 was no more and when she returned to the water on 1 October 1943, she was MTB 416. A few weeks later the famous 8th MGB Flotilla also came to an end. The order renumbering the flotilla arrived on 16 September and came into force on 15 October: from now on 416 would be part of the new 1st MTB Flotilla (the original 1st Flotilla, formed in March 1937 from the original 60ft British Power Boat MTBs, had disbanded in August 1942, by which time the obsolete boats, supported by a handful of Vospers, had reached the end of their useful lives).

The new identity did not, however, bring much practical change. MTB 416 was not equipped with torpedoes, nor it appears were many other boats in the flotilla. In fact, it is only MTB 414 (ex-MGB 77) that definitely had torpedo tubes fitted, and pictures of several of the flotilla's boats around the time of the Normandy landings reveal that they were not equipped with them either.

The new flotilla made a brief excursion to Ramsgate in October but returned to Dartmouth a few weeks later. At the same time, 416's skipper John Mallitte was taken ill and Eric Archer, now a lieutenant, took temporary command followed by Lieutenant C.C.P. Broadhurst with Sub Lieutenant Cameron Gough as his first lieutenant.

Another new arrival in the flotilla in the latter half of the year was young Sub Lieutenant Patrick Macnee. Macnee had studied acting before the war but in 1942 joined the Royal Navy as an ordinary seaman, before qualifying as an officer in the summer of 1943. His memories of his time at Dartmouth reveal something of the social side of operations:

After up to twelve hours at sea, our hearts were light when we returned to the welcoming shores of England. We'd invariably alight from our boats tired and quite drenched through, but after the luxury of a hot bath and a wholesome breakfast

ABOVE One of the two 20.3cm railway guns at Auderville-Laye, photographed after its capture by US forces on 11 July 1944. *(US Army/Public Domain)*

LEFT MTB 457: the forward 2-pounder has been replaced with a 6-pounder and the rear turret is a twin hand-operated mounting. Behind the torpedo tubes, splinter mats cover the wheelhouse to provide additional protection from enemy fire. *(Al Ross)*

served by smiling Wrens, our weariness seemed to recede and we settled down to the necessary administrative work with renewed vigour.

After the hectic schedule of a busy morning, we would grab a quick drink before drifting off to sleep between sheets that crackled with starch. Greatly refreshed, we'd rise around 5 pm so as to be on the boats by seven o'clock. If that night's operation was cancelled for any reason, then we'd go off to the Imperial Hotel in Torquay for some relaxation.

The Head Waiter at the Imperial was named Joseph, and he affected French and Serbo-Croatian origins. In fact he was a raucous cockney who ignored the rationing rules and served us enormous meals that were always rounded off with liqueurs and cigars we hadn't ordered. During one such evening I glanced around the table. 'Bussie' Carr, my commanding officer, Eric Archer, who would later succeed him, 'Cam' [Gough] who would later succeed Eric, 'Topline' Broadhurst, 'Pop' Beck, Jami Shadbolt, 'Stoo' Large, and so many other good friends were puffing cigars, downing the liqueurs and roaring with the sort of laughter that comes from wondering whether we would live to enjoy another such night.[6]

---

6   Macnee, 1988, pp. 129–30.

BELOW Although best known for playing Steed in *The Avengers*, Patrick Macnee (left) also starred alongside Anthony Quayle in the film *The Battle of the River Plate* in 1956, which told the story of the Royal Navy's pursuit of the German pocket battleship *Graf Spee*. Macnee's naval service was far more real in the Second World War. (Alamy)

Mallitte and Okey returned to MTB 416 in December, but it was only until the New Year. On 5 January 1944, 416 returned to Poole for a refit, this time to replace her Oerlikons. Her Mk V power-operated turret was removed, and a new lightweight Mk IX hand-operated mounting was installed in its place. The new mount included a mahogany platform for the gunner so that he could rotate the turret around 360 degrees. This platform was slightly wider than the wheelhouse, so was supported with chamfer boards below. The original turret had weighed nearly 700kg and the new one was less than half that, so there was no need for extra reinforcement.

When 416 returned to the water on 2 March it was with a new skipper. Lieutenant Gordon Lindsay Salmon took command, with Derek Okey remaining as first lieutenant. Lieutenant Commander Anthony Law remembered that Salmon was known, perhaps inevitably, as 'Fish', and that he 'sported a fair beard and a pair of twinkling blue eyes. True to those eyes, he was always up to some mischief, and when he hadn't a natter on he had a drip about something.'[7] The flotilla had a new CO as well. In January, Stephenson moved on and handed command back to John Mathias, who had held it previously in the wake of Hichens' death.

Preparing for the invasion

The 1st MTB Flotilla maintained its patrols of the Channel. Although the men didn't know it, they were one of many units suppressing the S-boats and guarding the huge number of ship movements along the south coast as the invasion fleet slowly assembled itself. Radar stations kept a constant vigil for S-boats and interceptions were frequent.

The 5th S-boat Flotilla's year had begun well, with a successful attack on convoy WP 457 sinking four ships and another on CW 243 sinking three. In February they were joined in Cherbourg by the 9th Flotilla, but soon the weight of Allied offensive patrols showed itself. Two operations in late February and four in March were beaten off by patrols

---

7   Law, 1989, p. 39.

or aircraft. In April it became even harder to cross the Channel and although the S-boats successfully attacked convoy T4, the ill-fated Exercise Tiger task force, no fewer than ten attempts to intercept convoys were beaten back by the Royal Navy. On the night of the 21st, that duty was performed by MTBs 414 and 416.

That night, ten S-boats of the 5th and 9th Flotillas sailed from Cherbourg to intercept convoy WP 510. Five boats of the 9th Flotilla headed into Lyme Bay, with the 5th patrolling further west. The 1st MTB Flotilla had two patrols at sea. In Lyme Bay, Force 113 was led by Lieutenant Francis Head on MTB 414 and supported by Salmon on 416, for what was only his second patrol in command. Head had begun his career as Hichens' first lieutenant in 1941 and remained with the flotilla until he was killed in a motorcycle accident in February 1945. Force 114 consisted of MTBs 430, 434 and 431 patrolling to the west in the vicinity of the Eddystone Rocks.

Arriving at their patrol location at 10:13pm, Force 113 cut their engines and 416 set up watch with their hydrophone equipment. This, it later transpired, was faulty, and when 414 took over at 1:00am, engines were immediately detected to the south-west. The engines continued north, passing to the west of the patrol and although they couldn't be seen or heard above water, the strength of the hydrophone reading indicated they were close.

Rather than draw attention to themselves, Head elected to wait until the enemy's intentions were clear. At 1:20am he was contacted by Lieutenant Richard Guy Fison, the Coastal Forces naval controller at Kingswear's Radar Control Unit. Using radio phone instead of telegraphy, Fison passed accurate bearings to Head and Force 113 started their engines and raced towards the enemy.

Fison continued to update Head on the enemy's location, nursing the MTBs into position until, at 1:34am, the enemy were sighted, revealing themselves to be five S-boats. Head later commented on their appalling station keeping, with the leading three boats in a line separated by at least 300m from the pair bringing up the rear.

A minute later, Head signalled to Fison 'Tally Ho' and the MTBs opened fire on the S-boats, concentrating on the fourth boat in line. The S-boats may have been expecting to meet another group of friendly boats (possibly the 5th Flotilla), as the MTBs were able to close to within 200m without the enemy responding. Even as gunfire arched across the sky towards them, the crew of S 167 hoisted a recognition signal. The MTBs punished them for this mistake and numerous hits registered from the Oerlikons and pom-poms of both boats.

As 414 led 416 in a curve to port to close on the stricken enemy boat, a shell suddenly thudded into 416's bow. Unable to complete the turn, Salmon instead turned to starboard and, noticing that the fourth and fifth S-boats were now firing on each other, continued his turn to make a second attack on them. Before he could make his approach, one of the crew alerted him to a fire in the mess deck. Salmon stopped and a fire party went below to deal with the damage.

Lying inert in the swell, 416's crew trained their guns on the damaged S-boat in the distance but held their fire – it wouldn't be wise to draw attention to themselves when they couldn't easily escape. Slowly the S-boat drifted out of sight. Below decks the firefighting team got the fire under control. There was 2ft of water in the mess deck, but thick smoke continued to billow out of the compartment, making it impossible to know how much damage had been caused. Salmon cautiously headed east at slow speed hoping to find his quarry again, but a few minutes later there was more bad news. He later reported that 'there was a hole, the size of a dinner plate, on the port side of the heads flat, and that water was entering the mess deck through a hole in the watertight bulkhead'.

Salmon increased speed to lift the bow out of the water and set off to find 414, guided by Fison on shore. Unable to locate him, Salmon turned for home instead; 414, meanwhile, had lost contact during the turn to port so set off instead after the leading three boats, which had opened their throttles in an attempt escape. Head watched with satisfaction as several shots hit the lead boat, but even at 40kts the S-boats were able to pull away and eventually he disengaged and headed for

Dartmouth, arriving at 3:45am, 25 minutes after 416.

The action was the first occasion in which a shore-based control station successfully vectored MTBs on to their target and led to significant damage to S 167. The British crews were elated by the German reaction – despite the odds, the S-boats were completely unwilling to mix it with the MTBs.

Nonetheless, 416 had suffered considerable damage in the bow and from the fire, damage that would warrant another visit to Poole. A few days later, MTBs 459 and 461 called into Dartmouth and together they sailed up the coast to Poole on 28 April; 459 was commanded by Salmon's friend, Anthony Law, whose boat also needed some minor repairs after their working-up at Holyhead.

At the entrance to Poole Harbour 461 left them and carried on to Shoreham, while Salmon and Law waited for a pilot to guide them in. After waiting for a while, Salmon became impatient. Knowing the harbour well, he decided to be his own pilot and together the two boats crept into the harbour and snaked their way along the meandering channels to the British Power Boat yard.

A few hours later, Law found himself in front of the Naval Officer in Charge. Ignoring their orders to wait was one thing, but more seriously the commander explained, the pilot had gone out of his way for nothing and had to pay his own petrol costs. Fortunately, Law and Salmon were able to solve this problem by taking the pilot to the Antelope Inn that night.

D-Day

MTB 416's repairs took a month, and she was lucky to be back in the water by 27 May, just over a week before D-Day. On her return to Dartmouth she received a new skipper once more; this time it was Cameron Gough with Sub Lieutenant George Baptie as his first officer. It was probably during the refit that she received some new equipment – a picture of 416 in June shows small racks along her deck and it's likely she was equipped to carry the same small Mk XII depth charges as the 29th (Canadian) MTB Flotilla.

The 1st MTB Flotilla remained at Dartmouth for the Assault Phase of D-Day. On the night of 5 June, MTBs from Plymouth Command patrolled to the south of the channels used by Force O and U (bound for Omaha and Utah respectively) to sail up from the West Country to the 'spout' that led south from the Isle of Wight and into the invasion area. S-boats did not seem to menace the Plymouth Command area, however, and a week later the first of the flotilla's boats began to make their way to HMS *Hornet* in Gosport, under Portsmouth Command. Their role in Lyme Bay was taken over by Fairmile MLs.

Less than two weeks after D-Day, with US forces closing from the south, the Kriegsmarine began to evacuate Cherbourg. On the night of 18 June, the S-boats of the 5th and 9th Flotillas sailed for the Channel Islands, closely guarded by shore batteries that prevented MTBs from getting close.

The S-boats escaped just in time. On the 19th a major storm blew over Normandy, wrecking one of the Allies' fragile Mulberry harbours and curtailing naval operations on both sides. By the 22nd the weather had eased

BELOW An MTB of the 29th (Canadian) MTB Flotilla sails between landing ships of the invasion fleet. *(Library and Archives Canada/PA-144576)*

LEFT Two Mk VI boats of the 29th (Canadian) MTB Flotilla. While the MTB has been re-equipped with torpedoes, the other boat is still fitted with racks full of Mk XII depth charges. *(Library and Archives Canada/ PA-144573)*

and on the night of 23/24 June, no fewer than 21 MTBs sailed from Portsmouth. Twelve were bound for Cherbourg and included boats from the 1st, 14th and 53rd MTB Flotillas organised into four units. GF2 was composed of three boats of the 1st MTB Flotilla – 430, 416 and 413. GF3 included 254, 255 and 257 and GF4 was made up of 250, 251 and 249, all of the 14th MTB Flotilla. GF5 included MTBs 693, 694 and 689, powerful Fairmile D Dog Boats of the 53rd MTB Flotilla.

At 12:25am on the 24th, control ship

BELOW MTB 416 leads boats of the 1st MTB Flotilla on their return from operations off the Normandy coast in June 1944. *(IWM A24047)*

HMS *Duff* plotted a convoy of seven vessels, escorted by several smaller craft, leaving Cherbourg and heading west. Undeterred by covering shellfire from coastal batteries, units GF2 and GF3 instantly roared into the attack, reaching the convoy just outside the breakwater where they were still forming up. For MTB 413, ex-MGB 75, this was a familiar scene – she had been with Hichens two years previously when the lack of torpedoes had so vexed the senior officer. This time, there were torpedoes aplenty and four were thought by the crews to have struck targets. At least one ship was seen to sink and three others left in a sinking condition.

Three ships escaped to the west where the MTBs of GF4 fell on to them, with several more hits and at least one ship sunk. A surviving coaster attempted to escape the net but was intercepted by the Dog Boats of GF5. Dodging

BELOW The grave of Able Seaman Thomas Walter Simpson. The inscription reads 'In remembrance. Gone from us but not forgotten, never shall thy memory fade.' *(Author)*

constantly, the coaster desperately sought to prevent the MTBs lining up a suitable torpedo shot, so in the end they closed and destroyed her with gunfire.

Their work done, the MTBs withdrew from the coast under constant harassing fire from the coastal batteries. In less than an hour they had successfully prevented any escapes from the port, but the battle was not entirely one-sided and among the MTBs were six casualties. Five men were wounded, but on board 416, one of the crew was killed.

Able Seaman Thomas Walter Simpson was a 21-year-old from Wapping, London. He had in fact just received a Distinguished Service Medal that had been gazetted (published in the *London Gazette*) only four days previously, 'for outstanding leadership, courage and skill in Light Coastal Craft'. He was taken ashore at HMS *Hornet* and shortly afterwards was laid to rest in Haslar Royal Naval Cemetery in Gosport, where no fewer than 531 sailors who lost their lives in the Second World War are buried. Simpson was the only fatal casualty suffered by MGB 81/MTB 416 during the war, but nonetheless, 416 sailed on patrol again the next night.

A month later, the crew of MTB 416, exhausted by constant operations, found the enemy again. During a patrol with 415 on the night of 18/19 July, the boats were vectored on to a small convoy of R-boats which they attacked and scored hits on. The R-boats returned in kind, however, and 416 suffered hull damage and wounds to the crew, including Gough. Command of 416 passed to a Canadian, Lieutenant Frederick Stewart Large.

The flotilla lost its commander as well. On the night of 26/27 July, Mathias on MTB 430 accompanied by 431 and Salmon on 412, intercepted six S-boats off Cap d'Antifer. As Mathias led his boats through the enemy's line, 430 was rammed by S 182 and blew up. Immediately behind, Salmon had no time to avoid the wreckage and piled into 430, suffering enough damage to sink her. Although Mathias survived the fireball that engulfed 430, he was wounded and 11 of his crew were killed. Salmon and all but one of his crew escaped from 412, but Derek Okey, MGB 81's former first lieutenant, was lost.

North for the final time

The Battle of Seine Bay continued until the land forces in Normandy broke out from the beachhead and advanced through France. At the end of August, the final Kriegsmarine units withdrew from the Channel, and the fight returned to the North Sea. So too did the 1st MTB Flotilla, who sailed to HMS *Mantis* at Lowestoft in September. Mathias had briefly been succeeded by Lieutenant John Bennet, but at Lowestoft Lieutenant Charles Thornycroft took command for the rest of the war. Very soon the flotilla found themselves on the familiar Z line defending against the new wave of S-boat attacks on east-coast shipping – but operations had changed in the North Sea and on 30 September, 416 and seven other boats were accompanied by a control frigate for a patrol of the sort they had become accustomed to in the Channel. She repeated the role on 2/3 and 15/16 October. MTB 416 quickly headed south again, though, undergoing a refit at Brightlingsea from 21 October to 29 November. At the same time Stewart Large returned to Canada and Lieutenant Kenneth Hughes became 416's skipper.

When she returned, the flotilla was back at HMS *Beehive*. She undertook patrols on 6/7, 7/8 and 11/12 December, but according to her service log, she then slipped for further repairs at Brightlingsea from 14 to 30 December. Curiously the operations log refers to her undertaking six patrols in this same period, including Christmas Day, so at least one of these is in error and it seems unusual for her to require a refit so soon after the last.

The New Year began in much the same way with regular patrols on 2/3, 6/7, 11/12, 17/18, 23/24, 24/25 and 30/31 January. In February, Hughes and Baptie left 416 to stand by a new boat – MTB 499 at British Power Boat – and

BELOW The aftermath of the disastrous fire at Ostend. The upturned hull of a Fairmile D on the right has been cut into in order to search for survivors. *(Library and Archives Canada/PA-116484)*

Sub Lieutenant D.L. Bailey took command. His first lieutenant was probably Patrick Macnee, as they both moved to British Power Boat together in May to commission MTB 506.

The 1st MTB Flotilla occasionally relocated across the North Sea to Ostend and on 14 February, 416 witnessed, but fortunately wasn't involved in, the largest disaster in Coastal Forces history. Thirty-two boats had been crammed into the narrow dock on the west side of the harbour mouth (now called Montgomerydok), when a fire broke out on the water's surface after petrol had leaked from one of the boats. The fire spread quickly and a few minutes later a tremendous explosion ensued. Sixty-four men were killed and twelve MTBs were destroyed, seven of them British Power Boat Mk V and Mk VIs. It was a devastating loss so close to the end of the war.

As it was, MTB 416's war was almost at an end. As one of the four surviving boats

of the first order of Mk V MGBs, she was now among the oldest boats still in service. She made patrols on 17/18, 19/20 and 27/28 February, but on 5 March, approval was received to lay her up as a Category C (poor condition) boat in reserve at Poole. That night she sailed on her final patrol in the North Sea, accompanied by MTBs 486, 490 and 491 – all newer Mk VI boats that now populated the flotilla.

End of service

MGB 81 arrived at Poole Harbour and was formally paid off (decommissioned) on 27 April 1945. She was taken in hand at British Power Boat's yard in the harbour on 10 May and stripped of her armaments and equipment before she was laid up in reserve.

The end of the war in the Far East brought with it a certainty that the majority of vessels that had served in Coastal Forces would no longer be required. The Admiralty gave approval to dispose of MGB 81 on 2 October and on the 25th she was handed over to the Director of Small Craft Disposals, Poole.

At some point in the following period she was sold to a Mr J. Evans, and for the next few years disappears from the record. She next pops up in 1958 when she was arrested for smuggling by Her Majesty's Customs at Shoreham-by-Sea. Arresting a ship might seem odd, but it is a normal step taken by HM Customs for maritime claims in the event of fines or charges being levied against the owners. The ship is then sold by the Admiralty Marshal to pay for the claims and cost of arrest. In MTB 416's case she was sold to a Gosport scrap dealer who stripped her of her machinery. She was then moved to Hardway in Gosport, a former embarkation hard used by landing ships on D-Day, and became an accommodation barge for the sailing school there. In the 1960s she was fitted out as a houseboat and moved to a mud berth at Quay Lane Marina, until she was purchased and named *Cresta* in 1984. The new owner towed her to Bursledon on the River Hamble, where she seemed likely to see out her final days.

ABOVE **MTB 482 flying her paying-off pennant, prior to being decommissioned.** *(Christopher Timms)*

LEFT **MGB 81 as the houseboat *Cresta*, Quay Lane Marina, Gosport, 1985.** *(David Fricker)*

Chapter Seven

Restoring MGB 81

MGB 81's story might have ended in the same way as so many other ex-Coastal Forces boats, were it not for the timely intervention of dedicated people with a genuine desire to see her restored to her former glory. It is thanks to their work over the course of many years that she was finally able to go to sea again.

OPPOSITE MGB 81 is lifted on to a low-loader for her move to the British Military Powerboat Trust yard in 1999. *(BMPT Collection, via PNBPT)*

151
RESTORING MGB 81

A new chapter

On 13 January 1988, Guy Webster purchased the houseboat *Cresta* from John Pepperell. After the passage of more than 40 years, her wartime identity was assumed but no longer certain. Close inspection of the hull revealed crucial details that confirmed her original name: carved on the stem inside the bow was the number 1807 (MGB 81's yard number) and scored into her transom the number 416 (her later MTB number). Remarkably, 1807 was also found in faint pencil on some timbers inside the hull.

Guy and his father Art Webster determined to restore *Cresta* to her wartime appearance, preferring her gunboat identity over MTB 416. With the decision made, her journey to complete restoration began, although it would be far from easy. Initially it was necessary to remove some 5 tons of non-original timber fittings inside her hull and more than a ton and a half of concrete and roofing felt from her deck. A custom-made cradle was built using wartime plans and by September 1988 she was out of the water on a slip at Bursledon Marina.

The hull was stripped back to bare wood for inspection and a small section of outer layer planking was replaced. Both chine timbers were renewed and the port gunwale was restored. On the deck, the entire houseboat-era deckhouse was removed, along with approximately 75% of the deck timbers. These were replaced and

BELOW **MGB 81 as the houseboat *Cresta*, shortly after her arrival at Bursledon in March 1986.** *(David Fricker)*

a new wheelhouse was built. New hatches and coamings were installed and a replica breakwater was put in place on the bow.

Below decks, several longitudinal girders were replaced and new bulkheads installed fore and aft of the fuel tank space and engine room. A hole was repaired in the steering compartment and new pillar supports were installed in the mess deck and engine room to better support the deck. Almost the entirety of the inside of the hull was stripped of decades of paint and recoated in damp seal paint and epoxy where necessary.

Before she returned to the water in 1990 her underwater hull was covered in epoxy and given a coat of antifoul. Above the waterline she received a new two-tone camouflage pattern for the first time since the war and new electrics were fitted throughout. Finally, replica weapons were installed on the deck.

A working boat

The Websters' work undoubtedly saved MGB 81 and reversed decades of neglect of her wartime fittings and layout, but she still lacked machinery. Further work prepared her to receive new engines, but in the mid-1990s she moved downriver to Crableck Marina at Sarisbury Green. Here she remained until 17 September 1998 when, more than 10 years after they had acquired her, the Websters sold MGB 81 to Philip Clabburn.

This was not the first British Power Boat that Philip had acquired. Eight years earlier he had purchased ST 206, one of the original seaplane tenders that Scott-Paine had built for the RAF in 1931. In 1992 he spotted the houseboat *Excervus* on the River Dart and recognised her as RAF HSL 102, one of British Power Boat's 64ft rescue boats. After founding Powerboat Restorations with his father Robin, Philip oversaw the restoration and relaunch of both in 1993 and 1996 respectively.

MGB 81 was moved to Marchwood Military Port and on 28 September left the water again. The boat's interior was stripped and the deck and wheelhouse, by now starting to deteriorate, were removed. A year later, on 23 September, she was moved to the British Military Powerboat Trust (BMPT) base at the former Husbands Shipyard at Cracknore Hard.

The BMPT was founded in 1999 with the aim of saving and restoring historic 20th-century military power boats and the long-term ambition of establishing a museum. Benefiting from Powerboat Restorations' expertise and the enthusiastic support of the trust's volunteers, restoration work on MGB 81 continued

ABOVE MGB 81 at the very start of her transformation. Initially this began as a new coat of paint, but later this saw her entire deck structure removed and a replica fitted in its place. *(David Fricker)*

BELOW MGB 81 as she appeared when taken on by Philip Clabburn. The Websters left her transom untouched where '416' had been scored into the wood. *(Danny Lovell)*

ABOVE MGB 81, her hull fully stripped, is lifted on to a low-loader for her move to the British Military Powerboat Trust yard. *(BMPT Archive, via PNBPT)*

ABOVE RIGHT MGB 81 had to be moved outside so that a crane could turn her over once the work on her hull was complete. *(BMPT Archive, via PNBPT)*

RIGHT Fabricating MGB 81's new wheelhouse. *(BMPT Archive, via PNBPT)*

RIGHT With the wheelhouse installed, the fitting-out of the boat could begin. *(BMPT Archive, via PNBPT)*

LEFT **The forward breakwater installed on the deck.** *(BMPT Archive, via PNBPT)*

LEFT **One of the three MAN diesel engines prior to installation in MGB 81's engine room.** *(BMPT Archive, via PNBPT)*

BELOW **MGB 81 takes to the water once again, 6 September 2002.** *(BMPT Archive, via PNBPT)*

ABOVE MGB 81 and Seaplane Tender 206 at the Southampton Boat Show shortly after her launch in 2002. Behind her is a replica of the *Endeavour*, the bark commanded by Captain Cook when he charted New Zealand and discovered the eastern coast of Australia. *(Tim Deacon)*

alongside several other Coastal Forces vessels, as well as those of the RAF and Army. Over the next couple of years, MGB 81's hull was professionally sandblasted inside and out and some damaged and non-standard lengths of the outer planking were replaced. At the start of the new millennium, work began on MGB 81's deck. New deck stringers were installed and it was completely replanked, while a brand new wheelhouse was constructed using original British Power Boat plans.

Efforts were made to source new engines. A set of original Packard marinised engines were located in Gibraltar, but it is dangerous – and expensive – to run petrol engines at sea. Instead, three reconditioned German MAN 1,000hp V12 turbo-diesel engines were installed in 2002. Once the machinery and electrics were fitted, MGB 81 received a fresh coat of paint to return her to her wartime scheme. On 6 September 2002 she was relaunched by Admiral Sir James Black (who had commanded the aircraft carrier HMS *Invincible* during the Falklands War) in the presence of her former skippers Eric Archer and Cameron Gough, along with James Shadbolt, another CO in the 1st MTB Flotilla.

At sea again

MGB 81 was a popular sight around the Solent and, in 2004, made her first trip back to Normandy in almost 60 years in order to attend the D-Day commemorations in June. Unfortunately, at home her future was not secure. The BMPT had been awaiting a longer lease on their site at Marchwood, but in 2003 it became clear that this would not become available and that the old Husbands yard would eventually be disposed of. Fortunately, Marchwood Military Port were able to offer some land on a short-term basis and on 30 September 2005 the last trust boat was moved out of Husbands yard. For several years the trust sought to find suitable new premises but without success. The future was bleak.

In 2009 a lifeline was thrown to the collection of boats at Marchwood. The BMPT chose to merge with the Portsmouth Naval Base Property Trust (PNBPT), the charity that runs Portsmouth Historic Dockyard at the south-west corner of HM Naval Base Portsmouth. The dockyard is home to the National Museum of the Royal Navy – with their historic vessels HMS *Victory*, HMS *Warrior* and HMS *M33* – and the *Mary Rose* Trust. BMPT assets, including many of their small boats, were transferred to PNBPT which, with the aid of a £580,000 grant from the National Heritage Memorial Fund and £170,000 from other sources, were also able to purchase MGB 81 and HSL 102 from Powerboat Restorations (ST 206 was sold to the RAF Museum in Hendon).

In 2010 MGB 81 moved to Portsmouth, initially at the marina alongside the Gunwharf Quays shopping centre and in the shadow of

the Spinnaker Tower. While a shopping centre might not seem a natural home for a gun boat, it was actually more than appropriate. In the summer of 1944, Gunwharf Quays was HMS *Vernon* and, with so many Coastal Forces craft crowded into Portsmouth Harbour, the present-day marina was the site of an additional mooring for MTBs based at HMS *Hornet* on the other side of the harbour.

That winter the boats moved round to new moorings beside HMS *Warrior* and behind Boathouse 4 in the historic dockyard. Over the next three years both received regular maintenance, annual lifts from the water to clean the hull, and some important improvements. HSL 102 was upgraded to be able to take passengers and conduct pleasure-cruising work, while MGB 81 was finally given some armament. Replica 20mm Oerlikon cannon were installed in a rear turret, a 2-pounder was fabricated for the bow and replica depth charges and Lewis guns were fitted on the deck. Each summer she visited Normandy for the D-Day commemorations, becoming a popular attraction at Pegasus Bridge on the Caen Canal.

A necessary overhaul

In June 2017, MGB 81 moved to the Berthon Boat Company yard in Lymington, Hampshire. Here she would undergo a substantial restoration and receive three new engines in her first major refit since her relaunch in 2002. The work was funded by the British government's LIBOR fund, created from 2013 fines levied at banks involved in manipulating exchange rates in London.

The planned restoration would be extensive. Although designed and built to an incredibly high standard by British Power Boat, wooden power boats undergo great stress when planing and require regular maintenance. By now, original timber frames were beginning to weaken, and the refurbished MAN engines were no longer operating to their full potential.

To return MGB 81 to full working order, the boat's major hull frames and stringers would be replaced, while timbers across the rest of the hull would be inspected and changed as

Just as in the 1940s, in order to remove and install engines, the rear sections of the wheelhouse needed to be taken off. *(PNBPT)*

necessary. The wheelhouse and deck would be serviced, repairs made to the deck hatches and below deck the interior cabin spaces would be refitted. Almost the entirety of MGB 81's machinery would be replaced – new fuel tanks and a supply system would fuel the modern Italian FPT Cursor 13 diesel engines, replacing the older German MAN engines. Additionally, 81 would receive new gearboxes, seawater cooling system and exhausts, new generators and batteries, new shafts and propellers and, on the bridge, new engine controls and displays. Finally, the entire boat would be repainted, including antifoul below the waterline.

Berthon was a very appropriate yard to carry out the work. In 1917 the company occupied the site of a much older boat yard in Lymington and built numerous pleasure boats and yachts, including small craft for the Admiralty. Between 1940 and 1945 the yard built numerous Motor Fishing Vessels (MFVs) and Landing Crafts Assault (LCAs) for the Royal Navy, as well as 37 Harbour Defence Motor Launches. In 1941 the yard received an

ABOVE The central hatch does not expose the wing engines. To remove these, access points in the deck allow strops (green) to be fitted to raise the engine off its beds. *(PNBPT)*

LEFT Once elevated, strops from the main hatch (red) are connected, and weight is slowly transferred to these. *(PNBPT)*

RIGHT As tension is increased on the red strops and decreased on the green, the engine slowly swings into the centre of the boat and can be raised through the hatch. *(PNBPT)*

ABOVE, ABOVE RIGHT AND RIGHT The layout of the engine room needed to be modified to accommodate the new engines. The longitudinal engine beds were reshaped to fit them, and bespoke brackets were created to support the central engine. *(PNBPT)*

additional order to construct six Vosper 70ft MTBs. Three of these boats served in Peter Dickens' 21st MTB Flotilla, alongside Robert Hichens' 8th MGB Flotilla and MGB 81 at HMS *Beehive* in Felixstowe.

Upon her arrival in Lymington on 26 June, MGB 81 was lifted out of the water and into the yard where she would remain for 16 months. Initially she was kept in the yard's M-Shed, built in the 1990s to replace the ageing pre-war sheds, and here was given time to dry out while a complete survey was made of her hull and fittings. In September she was moved to the neighbouring West Solent Shed where the restoration was carried out.

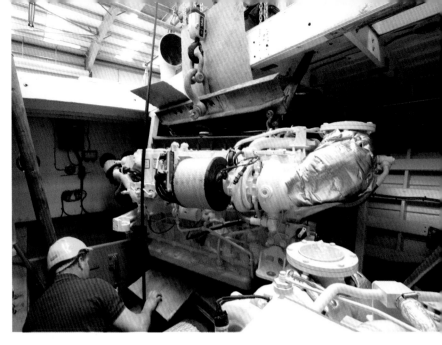

ABOVE As was the case during the removal of the old engines, the new engines were installed by transferring the weight from the main hatch strops to those passing through the access points. *(PNBPT)*

CENTRE AND LEFT To complement the engines, MGB 81 also received new shafts and new propellers. *(PNBPT)*

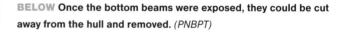

ABOVE Inside MGB 81's hull, a lot of frame timber, by now 75 years old, was starting to decay. The bottom beams in the forward half of the vessel needed to be replaced and, in order to do this, almost the entirety of the deck needed to be cleared. The deck panels and settee berth tops were lifted and stored, and the floor-bearers removed. *(PNBPT)*

LEFT AND BELOW LEFT The longitudinal girders that make up the forward part of the berths down each side of the hull also needed to be removed, to provide access to the chine and the biscuits joining the side beams to the bottom beams. *(PNBPT)*

BELOW Once the bottom beams were exposed, they could be cut away from the hull and removed. *(PNBPT)*

THIS PAGE New laminated beams were created at Berthon and, using the old beams as a guide, bent into the appropriate shape for each frame. Likewise, new biscuits were cut, based on the unique shape of each original one. *(PNBPT)*

ABOVE The hull would have been weakened if all the beams were removed at once, so they were replaced in groups before work moved along the hull. *(PNBPT)*

RIGHT With the beams in place, the new biscuits were inserted against the chine. *(PNBPT)*

BELOW AND RIGHT When MGB 81 was restored between 1998 and 2002, new outer timber longitudinal girders were installed along the port and starboard sides of the forward compartments, forming the front of the settee berths. However, these were separate 11ft 6in girders fore and aft of the bulkhead at frame 23. Because the girder did not continue through the bulkhead, the forward half of MGB 81 was not as stiff as it had been designed, and this produced a certain amount of flex in the hull. This in turn placed additional strain on the frames. To solve this, when the longitudinal girders were rebuilt, a scarf joint was used to join the timbers of the fore and aft girders to create one 23ft girder through the bulkhead. *(PNBPT)*

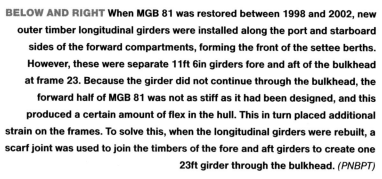

ABOVE To attach the new beams to the hull, they were screwed into place from outside the hull. To complete the work, the hull needed to be resealed. *(PNBPT)*

ABOVE RIGHT The hull was sanded and the screw heads were sealed with three layers of 300gsm cloth and epoxy resin. Green peel ply was added as a final layer to cure the epoxy and bring the amine compound to the surface. *(PNBPT)*

BELOW AND RIGHT With the epoxy resin cured, the green ply was removed. After another sanding, a final layer of epoxy paint was added. *(PNBPT)*

ABOVE AND ABOVE RIGHT After a final sanding, the entire hull was ready for a complete paint job. *(PNBPT)*

RIGHT AND BELOW MGB 81's light camouflage scheme was introduced to Coastal Forces in 1943. The lines were carefully masked before marine-grade paint was used on the hull, with black antifoul below the waterline. *(PNBPT)*

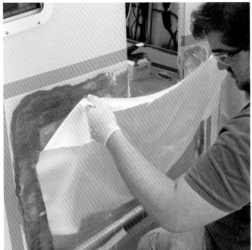

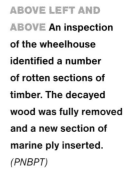

ABOVE LEFT AND ABOVE An inspection of the wheelhouse identified a number of rotten sections of timber. The decayed wood was fully removed and a new section of marine ply inserted. *(PNBPT)*

FAR LEFT AND LEFT As with the hull, 300gsm cloth and epoxy resin were layered over the ply to seal it. The surface was finished with green peel ply. *(PNBPT)*

LEFT Once the green peel ply was removed, the surface of the wheelhouse was ready to be sanded down and covered with a base coat, ready for the final painting. *(PNBPT)*

ABOVE MGB 81's instrument panel for her MAN engines also needed replacing. With three separate engines, all with individual displays, it was necessary to customise a brand-new panel. *(PNBPT)*

BELOW Each FPT Cursor 13 diesel engine had its own instrument panel, but three rectangular panels would not fit within the space between the gear levers on the port side of the wheel and the throttles on the starboard side. *(PNBPT)*

ABOVE The old dials were stripped out and the cables and wiring throughout the boat were replaced. *(PNBPT)*

BELOW Instead a brand-new instrument panel was custom made to fit the conning position. *(PNBPT)*

BELOW The dials were removed from their original panels and rewired into the panel from behind. *(PNBPT)*

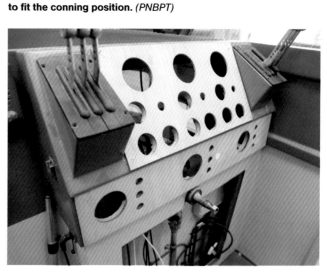

BELOW The finished panel. Each engine's revolutions are displayed on the main dial, with fuel, oil pressure, voltage and ignition switches below. *(PNBPT)*

LEFT AND BELOW
On 22 October 2018,
MGB 81 finally left the
West Solent Shed and
returned to the water.
(PNBPT)

Chapter Eight

The end of the gun boats

In total, 115 'short' boats and 79 'long' boats were commissioned as HM MGBs during the war. By the end of 1946 they had either been reclassified as MTBs, sold or sunk. Even the MTBs did not survive beyond 1949, when all Coastal Forces boats were reclassified as Fast Patrol Boats.

OPPOSITE The houseboat *Sungo*, ex-MTB 486, at Bitterne in Southampton. Launched in August 1944, this boat became leader of the 29th (Canadian) MTB Flotilla, under the command of Anthony Law. *(Author)*

In total, 39 Mk V and 50 Mk VI MGBs and
MTBs were built by British Power Boat during
the war. Most of these were completed by
the end of May 1945, but seven more (MTBs
507–509 and 519–522) were launched
between November 1945 and October 1946,
taking the total number of 71ft 6in boats to
leave the Hythe yard to 96. Although Coastal
Forces boats served in other theatres of war,
including the Mediterranean and the Bay of
Bengal, the British Power Boat Mk V and
Mk VIs served exclusively in home waters.

With the end of hostilities, first in Europe
and then in the Pacific, it was inevitable that the
Royal Navy would contract and the number of
MTBs far exceeded the peacetime need. Most
Coastal Forces boats, including the majority of
the British Power Boats, were paid off before
1945 was over.

Proud boats

The Royal Navy retained a small number
of boats from various yards at the end of
the war. Coastal Forces was overhauled and,
in recognition of the evolved nature of MTBs,
the new Fast Patrol Boat designation was
established in 1949. The retained boats were
recommissioned with a P prefix, bringing to an
end the life of the MTB.

New boats followed in 1952 with the *Gay*
class, built largely on the Vosper 73ft design
from the war. The boats could be equipped
either as torpedo boats or with higher-calibre
guns, essentially fulfilling the wartime roles of

the MTB or MGB. The *Gay* class was followed
a few years later by the *Dark* class, which
used aluminium frames and diesel engines,
a radical departure from the boats of only ten
years earlier.

Both classes were built in a number of
boat yards, including Vosper, Thornycroft and
Saunders Roe. Although British Power Boat
no longer survived, some of the company's
boats at least remained in Royal Navy
service. In 1949, 13 Mk VI British Power
Boats were recommissioned as Fast Patrol
Boats. These comprised some of the most
recently built boats – the oldest, MTB 470, was
commissioned in April 1944, but eight of them
had been commissioned between May 1945
and October 1946. In 1952, nine of these
were refitted as the *Proud* class of Fast Patrol
Boat, which outwardly differed little from the
original Mk VI.

Other boats also found new uses. Mk VI
MTBs 474, 481, 488, 490 and 499 were
converted to Control Target (CT) boats. As the
name implies, these were controlling vessels
for remote-controlled or towed targets that
other boats or aircraft could use for gunnery
practice. A few boats, including MTBs 454,
471, 472, 484 and 500 had the indignity
of being used as targets themselves. Five
boats (including some of the CT boats) were
converted to Radio Control Boats (RCBs)
in the late 1940s, although two of these
(both ex-Fast Patrol Boats) were considered
expendable targets as well.

Unfortunately, as a separate division of the

Royal Navy, Coastal Forces' days were also numbered. After the war, its bases around the country were closed, leaving only HMS *Hornet* in Gosport. This too was closed in 1957 and Coastal Forces essentially came to an end. Several of the Fast Patrol Boats were retained in local commands and for training, but the *Proud*-class boats were sold in 1958.

Houseboats

A very different future awaited the dozens of boats that had been paid off at the end of the war. In the age of sail, ships' commissions often lasted for as long as they served abroad at sea – perhaps a few years. To avoid desertion in other ports around the world, the crew weren't paid until they returned to Britain.

At their home port the overseas commission ended and the crew were literally 'paid off' as they departed the ship.

By the Second World War, the term paid off referred to the formal decommissioning of a ship, either to undergo a substantial refit or to be placed in reserve. For most it would be the last time the vessel served as a Royal Navy warship. It was usually a sad time for a crew too, as it marked the end of their time with the vessel and each other. The crew would be returned to manning stations and assigned to new vessels – it was unlikely that they would serve on the vessel or even alongside each other again.

Typically, the process began with formal approval from the Admiralty. The vessel made its final voyage to a suitable Royal Navy facility,

ABOVE **Another of Captain Morgan Cruises' boats was** *Raia*, **an unidentified 71ft 6in British Power Boat. She too was broken up in 2007.** *(Richard Hellyer)*

BELOW **MTB 102 remains well preserved today.** *(Richard Basey, MTB 102 Trust)*

often flying a paying-off pennant, a long narrow pennant to reflect the length of service the ship gave. On arrival at the port, the ship was formally decommissioned and the crew dispersed.

The boat was then stripped of equipment that could be reused on other vessels (such as weapons, wireless and radar). In the case of British Power Boat MTBs and MGBs this was sometimes done at Hythe, but most frequently at their facility in Poole Harbour. Once de-equipped the vessel was laid up – in the case of Coastal Forces vessels they were often removed from the water, although the sheer number of vessels decommissioned at the end of the war in Europe prevented this and many were left in trots on mud berths, floating with each incoming tide.

Once handed over to the local Director of Small Craft Disposals, the boat was invariably sold. Some were too old or badly damaged to be of future use and were sold cheaply to scrappers, but many found new futures. Some were acquired by local Sea Cadet units and others became pleasure boats. A large number became houseboats. Stripped of their engines and machinery and with new deckhouses fitted, a 70ft MTB was larger than most inner-city terraced houses. Around the country, harbours and marinas became home to a new type of houseboat. Fairmiles, Vospers and British Power Boats became comfortable homes for families for several decades.

Some boats became minor stars of the screen. MTB 102, Vosper's private venture and the ancestor of all their MTBs, was refurbished and made seaworthy again by a film company and used in the 1976 film *The Eagle Has Landed*, starring Michael Caine. Partially as a result of this timely intervention, 102 survives to this day in the care of the MTB 102 Trust.

No fewer than three ex-Coastal Forces craft starred in the 1955 film *The Ship that Died of Shame*, an Ealing Studios film based on a short story by Nicholas Monsarrat. The post-war *Gay*-class MTB *Gay Dragoon* and Vosper's MTB 528 briefly portrayed the fictional MGB 1087 in a few scenes, but the boat that depicted her throughout the bulk of the film was MTB 429, built by J.S. White in 1944. Although an MTB she later saw service in the

MTB 455

MTB 455 was originally ordered as MGB 136 but, after the redesignation of MGBs in 1943, she was launched as MTB 455 at the end of the year (albeit as a Mk V with a long wheelhouse). For the next year and a half she served in the 4th MTB Flotilla. Based in Lowestoft, she regularly made forays into the North Sea and, on the night of 14/15 February 1944, under the command of Lieutenant Rout RNZRN, she made a successful torpedo attack on an enemy armed trawler, which was sunk.

After she was placed on the disposal list in October 1945, she was sold. Some 70 years later she was the houseboat *Talisman*, moored on the River Itchen in Southampton at a mud berth in the shelter of St Denys railway bridge, only a few miles from where she was launched at Hythe.

After she was put up for sale in early 2018, she was moved downriver to a mud bank near Northam Bridge. Unfortunately, one day in September she began to leak and flooded as the tide came in. Had she been taken out of the water then it might have proved possible to save her, but it was sadly not to be. At each high tide her decks are awash. After less than a year her green hull and red deck have been turned almost black by algae and her frames and keel are waterlogged. Literally nothing can be salvaged from a boat when she is this far gone – eventually her hull will collapse or she will be broken up.

RIGHT, TOP MTB 455 in mid-2018, shortly after she moved to her new berth on the River Itchen. *(Author)*

RIGHT, CENTRE Four months later she flooded at high tide. *(Author)*

RIGHT, BOTTOM By the end of 2019, 455's hull had become rotten. It would be impossible to save any original features now. *(Author)*

RIGHT The fate of many boats, including MGB 81, was to wait to be purchased on the shore in Poole Harbour. *(Bernard Morgan, via Christopher Timms)*

Free Polish Navy as MTB S-10, but minus her torpedo tubes and in effect an MGB.

Some boats saw more active use. MTB 506, which was recommissioned as P 1506 and then as *Proud Grenadier*, was purchased by Southern Television in the early 1960s. Renamed *Southerner*, and refitted with gas turbine engines, she served as the television company's dedicated outside-broadcast boat. She covered notable events in the English Channel in the 1960s and '70s before Southern Television ceased broadcasting in 1982; 506 subsequently found her way to Malta where she operated as a ferry for Captain Morgan Cruises in Malta, under the name *Ambra*. Surprisingly enough she joined another (unfortunately unidentified) 71ft 6in British Power Boat run by the company and called *Raia*. Sadly, both boats were broken up in 2007.

Dwindling survivors

BELOW Ex-Mk VI MTB 506 (and later *Proud Grenadier*) assumed as new life as Southern Television's outside broadcasting boat *Southerner* in the 1960s and 70s. *(Richard de Kerbrech)*

Today there are far fewer houseboats than there were in the post-war period. Floating homes are harder to maintain than houses and few could be serviced as often as they should have been. As the boats aged, many became less habitable and the younger generations of the families that called them home moved ashore. Many boats became too weak to move and sank at their moorings before they were completely broken up. In the 1960s,

a large collection of wartime boats that had become part of a community of houseboats in Christchurch Harbour were forced to lease their moorings as a result of pollution concerns. Many were broken up on site, their remains burnt so that metal fittings could be salvaged.

At the end of 2019, there were believed to be a mere 29 surviving boats around the

ONE ANSWER to the housing problem may lie on the sands of Poole, Dorset, where these "little ships" have been put on the retired list. See story below . . .

'LITTLE SHIP' AS BUNGALOW HOME

By A. V. SELLWOOD

WANT to buy a bungalow? Why not buy one that floats?

Yesterday I went to Poole and saw, in narrow creeks and inlets, the Navy's most tragic spectacle of Britain—no longer needed to fight in Europe, unsuitable for the war against Japan—Ile huddled in funeral file along the mud off Shipstal Point.

Soon the little ships—I saw 127 of them—will be up for sale.

But they may fulfil a more noble purpose than providing scrap for the broker's yard.

Out of their hulls can be carved pleasant and spacious post-war homes. Officers proudly showed me Motor Torpedo Boat 685.

No. 685 is now their accommodation ship. She houses over 40 officers and men.

Engine-Room Lounge

Her radio room has been altered to hold a luxury bath and shower, two tanks have been removed—two bedrooms take their place. Where twin 1,500-h.p. engines raced against the swell in heat and clamour there is now a quiet, well-lighted lounge.

The ward-room, stripped of bunks, holds a dining-room and a set of chairs. And there is still ample space forward.

The galley has the amenities of a modern kitchen. Its fittings include a two-gallon electric urn and an elec-

tric geyser. Its serving hatch opens on the "dining-room."

There is plenty of cupboard room—provided by the former magazine.

The cost of reconversion? Lieut. F. M. Shore, D.S.C., and Bar, estimates that a "short" MTB—the class to which 685 belongs—could be fitted as a floating home for a family of five for anything between £200 and £1,000.

It depends on the degree of luxury you want. The joy of these things is that you can carve them up and add to them when and how you like.

The sales are controlled by the Director of Small Craft Disposals. Whether the little ships will go to the scrap heap or be turned into homes depends on the prices offered. They will go to the highest bidder.

Among officers like Lieut. Shore, who wish to live in the ships in which they fought and served.

ABOVE The houseboat *Laguna*, ex-MTB 490, at Shoreham-by-Sea. There is a community of 40 houseboats in Shoreham of which approximately half are former military boats. Twelve of these were Coastal Forces MTBs and MGBs. *(Author)*

ABOVE RIGHT The houseboat *Bimini*, ex-MTB 481, at Shoreham-by-Sea. Although the structures on the deck of converted MTBs and MGBs vary from one houseboat to another, the hull and bow are quite distinctive. *(Author)*

RIGHT MA/SB 27, a 63ft British Power Boat, takes to the water in May 2019 after an extensive restoration. She and MGB 81 are the only Coastal Forces British Power Boats in running order. *(Author)*

UK that served in Coastal Forces during the Second World War. The majority of these were houseboats (in varying condition) but there were at least three vessels in museum collections, three undergoing restoration and four that had been restored to seagoing condition. Incredibly, of the 29 survivors, no fewer than 13 were British Power Boats, the highest number of surviving vessels by any one boatbuilder. Eleven British Power Boats survived as houseboats and included nine Mk V or Mk VI boats and two 70ft whalebacks. Added to these are two restored boats, 63ft whaleback MA/SB 27 and MGB 81.

RIGHT MGB 81. *(PNBPT)*

List of British Power Boat Mk V

Class	Motor Gun Boat	Motor Torpedo Boat	Fast Patrol Boat	*Proud* Class	Control Target	Radio Control Boat
71ft 6in Mk V	MGB 74	MTB 412				
71ft 6in Mk V	MGB 75	MTB 413				
71ft 6in Mk V	MGB 76					
71ft 6in Mk V	MGB 77	MTB 414				
71ft 6in Mk V	MGB 78					
71ft 6in Mk V	MGB 79					
71ft 6in Mk V	MGB 80	MTB 415				
71ft 6in Mk V	MGB 81	MTB 416				
71ft 6in Mk V	MGB 107	MTB 417				
71ft 6in Mk V	MGB 108	MTB 418				
71ft 6in Mk V	MGB 109					
71ft 6in Mk V	MGB 110					
71ft 6in Mk V	MGB 111	MTB 430				
71ft 6in Mk V	MGB 112	MTB 431				
71ft 6in Mk V	MGB 113	MTB 432				
71ft 6in Mk V	MGB 114	MTB 433				
71ft 6in Mk V	MGB 115	MTB 434				
71ft 6in Mk V	MGB 116	MTB 435				
71ft 6in Mk V	MGB 117	MTB 436				
71ft 6in Mk V	MGB 118	MTB 437				
71ft 6in Mk V	MGB 119	MTB 438				
71ft 6in Mk V	MGB 120	MTB 439				
71ft 6in Mk V	MGB 121	MTB 440				
71ft 6in Mk V	MGB 122	MTB 441				
Prototype VI	MGB 123	MTB 446				
71ft 6in Mk V	MGB 124	MTB 442				
71ft 6in Mk V	MGB 125	MTB 443				
71ft 6in Mk V	MGB 126	MTB 444				
71ft 6in Mk V	MGB 127	MTB 445				
71ft 6in Mk V	MGB 128	MTB 447				
71ft 6in Mk V	MGB 129	MTB 448				
71ft 6in Mk V	MGB 130	MTB 449				
71ft 6in Mk V	MGB 131	MTB 450				
71ft 6in Mk V	MGB 132	MTB 451				
71ft 6in Mk V	MGB 133	MTB 452				
71ft 6in Mk V	MGB 134	MTB 453				
71ft 6in Mk V	MGB 135	MTB 454				
71ft 6in Mk V	MGB 136	MTB 455				
71ft 6in Mk V	MGB 137	MTB 456				
71ft 6in Mk V	MGB 138	MTB 457				RCB 8201 (194
71ft 6in Mk VI		MTB 458				
71ft 6in Mk VI		MTB 459				
71ft 6in Mk VI		MTB 460				
71ft 6in Mk VI		MTB 461				

Fate in service	Last known use
Sunk, 26/27 July 1944	
Disposal List, October 1945	
Sunk, 6 October 1942	
Disposal List, October 1945	
Sunk, 3 October 1942	
Sunk, 28 February 1943	
Disposal List, October 1945	
Disposal List, October 1945	Restored and operational, Portsmouth Historic Dockyard
Sunk 15/16 March 1944	
Disposal List, October 1945	
Badly damaged by mine, 7 February 1943. Not repaired	
Sunk, 29 May 1943	
Sunk, July 1944	
Disposal List, March 1945	
Disposal List, October 1945	
To Royal Netherlands Navy	
Sunk, 9 July 1944	
Disposal List, October 1945	
Disposal List, October 1945	
Disposal List, October 1945	Houseboat Fontenay, Hayling Island
Destroyed by Fire, 14 February 1945	
Disposal List, October 1945	Houseboat The Clive, Shoreham
Disposal List, October 1945	
Badly damaged by friendly fire, 23 October 1944. Not repaired	
Disposal List, January 1946	
Disposal List, October 1945	
Disposal List, April 1945	
Destroyed by Fire, 14 February 1945	
Disposal List, October 1945	
Disposal List, December 1945	
Sunk, 10 June 1944	
Disposal List, May 1948	
Disposal List, October 1945	
Disposal List, 1946	
Disposal List, June 1945	
Disposal List, January 1946	
Assigned to Target Trials, September 1946	
Disposal List, October 1945	Houseboat Talisman, Southampton. Sunk, 2018
Disposal List, October 1945	Houseboat Nokomis, Shoreham
Sold, October 1958	
Disposal List, February 1946	
Destroyed by Fire, 14 February 1945	
Sunk, 1 July 1944	
Destroyed by Fire, 14 February 1945	

Class	Motor Gun Boat	Motor Torpedo Boat	Fast Patrol Boat	*Proud* Class	Control Target	Radio Control Boat
71ft 6in Mk VI		MTB 462				
71ft 6in Mk VI		MTB 463				
71ft 6in Mk VI		MTB 464				
71ft 6in Mk VI		MTB 465				
71ft 6in Mk VI		MTB 466				
71ft 6in Mk VI		MTB 467				
71ft 6in Mk VI		MTB 468				
71ft 6in Mk VI		MTB 469				
71ft 6in Mk VI		MTB 470	P 1570 (1948)			
71ft 6in Mk VI		MTB 471				
71ft 6in Mk VI		MTB 472				
71ft 6in Mk VI		MTB 473				
71ft 6in Mk VI		MTB 474			CT 47 (1945)	
71ft 6in Mk VI		MTB 475				
71ft 6in Mk VI		MTB 476				
71ft 6in Mk VI		MTB 477				
71ft 6in Mk VI		MTB 478				
71ft 6in Mk VI		MTB 479				
71ft 6in Mk VI		MTB 480	P 1580 (1948)			RCB 8204
71ft 6in Mk VI		MTB 481			CT 48 (1945)	
71ft 6in Mk VI		MTB 482				
71ft 6in Mk VI		MTB 483				
71ft 6in Mk VI		MTB 484				
71ft 6in Mk VI		MTB 485				
71ft 6in Mk VI		MTB 486				
71ft 6in Mk VI		MTB 487				
71ft 6in Mk VI		MTB 488	P 1588 (1948)			RCB 8205
71ft 6in Mk VI		MTB 489				
71ft 6in Mk VI		MTB 490			CT 49 (1945)	
71ft 6in Mk VI		MTB 491				
71ft 6in Mk VI		MTB 492				
71ft 6in Mk VI		MTB 493				
71ft 6in Mk VI		MTB 494				
71ft 6in Mk VI		MTB 495				
71ft 6in Mk VI		MTB 496	P 1596 (1948)	*Proud Patriot* (1952)		
71ft 6in Mk VI		MTB 497				
71ft 6in Mk VI		MTB 498	P 1598 (1948)	*Proud Patroller* (1952)		
71ft 6in Mk VI		MTB 499			CT 46 (1945)	RCB 8202
71ft 6in Mk VI		MTB 500				
71ft 6in Mk VI		MTB 501				
71ft 6in Mk VI		MTB 502				
71ft 6in Mk VI		MTB 503				
71ft 6in Mk VI		MTB 504				
71ft 6in Mk VI		MTB 505	P 1505 (1948)	*Proud Fusilier* (1952)		
71ft 6in Mk VI		MTB 506	P 1506 (1948)	*Proud Grenadier* (1952)		
71ft 6in Mk VI		MTB 507	P 1507 (1948)	*Proud Guardsman* (1952)		
71ft 6in Mk VI		MTB 508	P 1508 (1948)	*Proud Highlander* (1952)		
71ft 6in Mk VI		MTB 509	P 1509 (1948)	*Proud Knight* (1952)		
71ft 6in Mk VI		MTB 519	P 1519 (1948)	*Proud Lancer* (1952)		
71ft 6in Mk VI		MTB 520				
71ft 6in Mk VI		MTB 521	P 1521 (1948)			RCB 8203 (195
71ft 6in Mk VI		MTB 522	P 1522 (1948)	*Proud Legionary* (1952)		

Fate in service	Last known use
Destroyed by Fire, 14 February 1945	
Sunk, 7 July 1944	
Badly damaged in fire, 14 February 1945. Not repaired	
Destroyed by Fire, 14 February 1945	
Destroyed by Fire, 14 February 1945	
Disposal List, September 1945	Houseboat *Platypus*, Hayling Island
Disposal List, January 1947	
Disposal List, July 1946	
Broken up, February 1952	
Assigned to Target Trials, 1946. Disposal List, May 1948	
Assigned to Target Trials, September 1946	
Disposal List, September 1945	
Disposal List, May 1947	
Disposal List, 1946	
Disposal List, December 1945	
Disposal List, November 1945	Houseboat *Shearwater*, Southampton
Disposal List, November 1945	
Disposal List, October 1945	
Sunk, 23 August 1956 in Malta	
Disposal List, May 1947	Houseboat *Bimini*, Shoreham
Disposal List, September 1945	
Disposal List, June 1945	
Assigned to Target Trials, 1946. Disposal List, 1947	
Disposal List, 1948	
Disposal List, 1946	Houseboat *Sungo*, Southampton
Disposal List, September 1945	Houseboat *Venture*, Shoreham
Sold, October 1948	
Allegedly sunk in experiments at Loch Striven, 1947	
Disposal List, January 1948	Houseboat *Laguna*, Shoreham
Disposal List, January 1946	
Disposal List, February 1946	
Badly damaged in action, 7 April 1945. Not repaired	
Sunk, 7 April 1945	
Disposal List, September 1945	
Sold, June 1958	
Disposal List, February 1946	
Sold, June 1958	
Sold, October 1958	
Assigned to Target Trials, 1946. Disposal List, October 1948	
Disposal List, September 1945	
Disposal List, September 1947	
Sold, February 1948	
Sold, February 1948	
Sold, June 1958	
Sold, June 1958	TV boat *Southerner*, later Malta ferry *Ambra*. Broken up 2007
Sold, June 1958	
Sold, June 1958	
Sold, June 1958	
Sold, 1958	
Sold, July 1948	
Sold, October 1958	
Sold, June 1958	

Types of MGBs in RN service during the Second World War

Pennant numbers	Total number	Constructor	Hull length	Notes
6–21	16	British Power Boat	70ft	Converted MA/SBs
40–45	6	British Power Boat	63ft	Originally ordered as Swedish and Norwegian MTBs: T1–2 and MTB 1–4
46	1	British Power Boat	70ft	Originally ordered as Dutch MTB: TMB 51
47–48	2	J. Samuel White	75ft 6in	Originally ordered as Polish MTBs
50–67	18	British Power Boat	70ft	Originally ordered as French MTBs: VTB 34–40
68–73	6	Higgins	69ft	Early Higgins Industries PT boats provided to Britain under Lend-Lease
74–81	8	British Power Boat	71ft 6in	Mk V MGBs. First purpose-built MGBs
82–93	12	Elco	70ft	Elco boats produced to the same design as British Power Boat 70ft boats and provided to Britain under Lend-Lease
98–99	2	A.C. de la Loire, Nantes	65ft 7in	French VTBs 13 and 14 that escaped after the fall of France
100–106	7	Higgins	69ft	Early Higgins Industries PT boats provided to Britain under Lend-Lease
107–127	21	British Power Boat	71ft 6in	Mk V MGBs. MGBs 128–138 were completed as MTBs 447–457 and all subsequent boats were completed as Mk VI MTBs
177–192	16	Higgins	78ft	Ex-US PT boats of the 15th MTB Flotilla. In October 1944 these boats were stripped of their torpedoes and handed over to the Royal Navy in the Mediterranean

In total 115 'short' MGBs were commissioned into the Royal Navy. A further 79 'long' MGBs were built by Fairmile and Camper & Nicholson.

RIGHT MGB 100, a 69ft Higgins supplied to Britain under Lend-Lease *(Peter Scott)*

Bibliography and sources

Although not as widely celebrated as the battleships and destroyers of the Second World War, there are several books that tell the story of Coastal Forces. Peter Scott's *The Battle of the Narrow Seas*, written during the war and published at its conclusion, remains one of the classic accounts of small-boat warfare in the English Channel and North Sea. A more recent book that benefits from access to German accounts is *Home Waters MTBs & MGBs at War* by Leonard Reynolds, whose own wartime memoir, *Motor Gunboat 658*, remains a classic account of service on Fairmile Ds in the Mediterranean. *Coastal Forces at War* by David Jefferson, also published by Haynes, is another well-written and -illustrated history.

Many flotilla commanders put pen to paper to record their experiences in Coastal Forces after the war. Peter Dickens' *Night Action* is a classic account of MTB warfare and Anthony Law's *White Plumes Astern* is a definitive history of the 29th (Canadian) MTB Flotilla. Robert Hichens' record of his wartime experiences, *We Fought Them in Gunboats*, was published posthumously in 1944 after his death the year before. A fuller biography, using extensive material from *We Fought Them in Gunboats*, as well as personal diaries, was written by his son, Anthony, in 2007. An equally good biography of Hubert Scott-Paine was penned by Adrian Rance in *Fast Boats & Flying Boats*.

Al Ross and the late John Lambert published two volumes of detailed technical histories of Fairmile and Vosper boats, packed with construction details and technical drawings. A third volume is expected soon. Brice and Phelan's book is an excellent narrative of the evolution of small fast boats, and Lawrence Patterson, Hans Frank and W.J. Whitley have all produced excellent histories of German *Schnellboote*.

Brice, Martin & Phelan, Keiren, 1977. *Fast Attack Craft: The Evolution of Design and Tactics*. Macdonald & Janes.

Cobb, David, 1971. *Warship Profile 7: HM MTB Vosper 70 ft (British Motor Torpedo Boats)*. Profile Publications Ltd.

Dickens, Peter, 1974. *Night Action*. Seaforth Publishing.

Fock, Harald, 1978. *Fast Fighting Boats, 1870–1945: Their Design, Construction and Use*. Nautical Publishing Co. Ltd.

Foynes, J.P., 1994. *The Battle of the East Coast (1939–1945)*. Self-published.

Frank, Hans, 2007. *German S-Boats: In Action in the Second World War*. Seaforth Publishing.

Hichens, Anthony, 2007. *Gunboat Command*. Pen & Sword.

Hichens, Robert, 1944. *We Fought Them in Gunboats*. Michael Joseph Limited.

Holman, Gordon, 1943. *The Little Ships*. Hodder & Stoughton.

Holt, William, 1947. 'Coastal Forces Design'. *Transactions of the Institute of Naval Architects, 1947*. Republished in 1983 in *Selected Papers on British Warship Design in World War II*. Conway Maritime Press.

Jea, Tom, 1998. *MTB 102: Vosper's Masterpiece*. Friends of MTB 102.

Jefferson, David, 2008 (second edition). *Coastal Forces at War*. Haynes Publishing.

Konstam, Angus, 2010. *British Motor Gun Boat 1939–45*. Osprey.

Lambert, John, 1985. *Anatomy of the Ship: The Fairmile D Motor Torpedo Boat*. Conway Maritime Press.

Lambert, John & Ross, Al, 1990. *Allied Coastal Forces of World War II, Volume 1: Fairmile Designs & US Submarine Chasers*. Conway Maritime Press.

Lambert, John & Ross, Al, 1993. *Allied Coastal Forces of World War II, Volume 2: Vosper MTBs & US ELCOs*. Conway Maritime Press.

Lenton, H.T. & College, J.J., 1963. *Warships of WWII, Part 7: Coastal Forces*. Ian Allan Ltd.

Macnee, Patrick, 1988. *Blind in One Ear*. Virgin Books.

Menzies, Ian, 2012. *We Fought Them on the Seas*. The Cheshire Press.

Patterson, Lawrence, 2015. *Schnellboote: A Complete Operational History*. Seaforth Publishing.

Pickles, Harold (ed.), 1994. *Untold Stories of Small Boats at War*. The Pentland Press Ltd.

Pink, Brian, 2005. *Wartime Exploits of Coastal Forces Craft built at Berthon Boat Company, Lymington, 1939–1945*. St Barbe Museum & Art Gallery.

Rance, Adrian, 1989. *Fast Boats & Flying Boats*. Ensign Publications.

Reynolds, Leonard, 2000. *Home Waters MTBs & MGBs at War*. Sutton Publishing.

Scott, Peter, 1945. *The Battle of the Narrow Seas*. Country Life.

Scott, Peter, 1961. *The Eye of the Wind: An Autobiography*. Hodder & Stoughton.

Selman, Sarah, 2000. 'The Spitfires of the Sea'. *Powerboat*. British Military Powerboat Trust.

Seymour, Philip, 1995. *Where the Hell is Africa? Memoirs of a Junior Naval Officer in the Mid-Twentieth Century*. The Pentland Press.

Smith, Geoff, 1991. *The British Power Boat Company, Hythe, Hampshire. Personal Recollections*. Totton & Eling Historical Society.

Smith, Peter C., 1984. *Hold the Narrow Sea: Naval Warfare in the English Channel, 1939–1945*. Moorland Publishing.

Whitley, M.J., 1992. *German Coastal Forces of World War II*. Arms & Armour Press.

Index